BE'ER HAGOLAH INSTITUTES

293 Neptune Avenue
Brooklyn, New York 11235

"What I wouldn't have given to have been at home with my family, sitting at the Shabbos table and singing zemiros. But sometimes we must make sacrifices. And to enable even one Jew to come to these shores and celebrate Shabbos in freedom . . . . for that, my friends, any sacrifice is worthwhile."

Rabbi Avraham Kalmanowitz, *To Save A World*, Page 109

In our generation, thousands of Russian children are landing on American shores each year. And it is now up to us to make the sacrifices.

Be'er Hagolah Institutes was founded ten years ago to combat the forces that were preventing the ideals of Judaism from reaching the *neshamos* of these innocent children. There are presently close to 600 students studying at our school. This number is increasing dramatically each year as a result of the tremendous influx of new Soviet immigrants. Be'er Hagolah's outstanding staff of teachers, guidance counselors, family educators, and professionals offer a full range of educational programs for the students and their parents, as well as social experiences such as family *shabbatonim*, *chavrusa* programs with *bnei yeshivah*, Big Sister-Little Sister, Bais Yaakov pro grams, summer camping and countless other acti￼￼ geared to introduce and inspire them to To￼￼

"Each generation must answer to ￼ generation will have to give testimony reg￼ for Russian Jews."

Harav Hagaon R' Yaako￼ ￼￼netsky *zt"l*

Published and distributed
in the U.S., Canada and overseas by
C.I.S. Publishers and Distributors
180 Park Avenue, Lakewood, New Jersey 08701
(201) 905-3000 Fax: (201) 367-6666

Distributed in Israel by
C.I.S. International (Israel)
Rechov Mishkalov 18
Har Nof, Jerusalem
Tel:02-538-935

Distributed in the U.K. and Europe by
C.I.S. International (U.K.)
1 Palm Court, Queen Elizabeth Walk
London, England N16
Tel: 01-809-3723

Book and cover design: Deenee Cohen
Typography: Shami Reinman and Nechamie Miller

ISBN 1-56062-060-9 hard cover
1-56062-061-7 soft cover

PRINTED IN THE UNITED STATES OF AMERICA

PROFILES IN HOLOCAUST RESCUE

TO SAVE A WORLD

DR.
DAVID
KRANZLER

RABBI
ELIEZER
GEVIRTZ

CIS

P·U·B·L·I·S·H·E·R·S

New York · London · Jerusalem

In Memory of

Reb Elimelech Gavriel Tress זצ"ל

whose מעשים live on,

and will never be forgotten

משפחת טרעס

In loving memory
of my dear husband

Stephen S. Reich

of blessed memory

Claire Reich

לזכרון עולם ולעילוי נשמות הטהורים

כבוד אבי מורי ואמי מורתי

ר׳ מאיר שרייבער, ע״ה

ורעיתו, טרוילע (Therese) שרייבער, ע״ה

Rare individuals, who, like the heroes described in this book, fought with courage and אמונה to save and shield lives in our native Pressburg during the war; and whose boundless fortitude and warmth provided hope and nourishment to the shattered young people returning to, and passing through, Pressburg in search of themselves and their families after the war.

ולזכרון נצח לאחיותי

יענטיל (Juci) שרייבער, ע״ה

נענא (Nina) שרייבער ע״ה

who were torn from our family in Pressburg, and killed in Birkenau,

על קידוש השם

Mrs. Esther Oppenheimer
and family

THE BE'ER HAGOLAH STORY

"I want to enroll my daughter."

"What school did your daughter attend previously?"

"When I came from the Soviet Union, I went to a Yeshiva but had no money so I put her in a public school. But then I saw public school is bad - knives and drugs, so I put her into St. Sergius Academy."

The girl was asked if she was taken to church as part of her education. "Only on holidays, I went about four times, but every day we prayed in the room in the morning. The Jewish kids could just stand and listen."

She was asked if she knows what Shabbos is - No, she doesn't know. Her Jewish name? - No. Her mother interrupts. - "Are you going to punish her and not take her into your school? St. Sergius is full of Jewish children. It's the Jews' fault that they are there. Why could I not send my child to a yeshiva five years ago?"

Ten years ago, Be'er Hagolah Institute was founded under the auspices of leading Roshei Yeshiva, to reach the highly impressionable Russian children as soon as they arrive, and point them in the direction of Yiddishkeit. By beginning with the rudiments of Torah, the school works to strengthen their knowledge and commitment, so that the children can ultimately be placed in mainstream yeshivos and Bais Yaakov - type schools.

Little Marina came home from school a week before Pesach and begged her mother to rid the apartment of chometz. Marina's mother staunchly refused to allow any such foolishness. Undaunted, the girl thoroughly cleaned her own room and declared it off limits to the rest of her family. At the start of Pesach, she locked herself into her bedroom, for fear of even seeing chometz, and subsisted solely on the single box of matzos which she had received in school.

The key to improving the lives of many of these youngsters is to provide a Jewish education for their parents, as well. Aside from a full range of Judaic and secular study programs for children from nursery school through high school, Beer Hagolah also offers evening adult education classes, holiday programs and family shabbatonim to instruct and guide the parents of the students.

Most poignant, however, are the tales of the children, even first graders, teaching their parents that which they have learned in schools. They are bittersweet reminders of how little the adults know, how much the children have gained, and how bright their future can be.

It was the third time in one week that Sonya came to school without her Chumash. She had been warned time and again that she must bring it with her each day, but to no avail. The teacher remonstrated with the girl once again and demanded an explanation for her negligence. Shamefacedly, Sonya blurted out, "It's my father! I think he borrows my Hebrew books at night when I am sleeping and forgets to return them. Can I help it if he wants to learn too?"

☆   ☆   ☆

The office received a call from the Steins, who volunteered to host a Russian family for the two Sedarim. It seemed that the family spent the first Pesach Seder at the Steins', but failed to attend the second. Concerned about the welfare of their guests, the hosts contacted the school to inquire about the situation. When questioned as to what happened, the Russian child responded, "My parents didn't feel comfortable attending a second Seder." When asked why she didn't attend the Seder herself, her face registered a look of surprise. "But I had to be home to show my parents what to do!"

☆   ☆   ☆

Erev Chanukah, the students of Beer Hagolah were dismissed after being equipped with menorahs and candles, fully prepared to celebrate the holiday. The following day in school, the second grade teacher asked her students to recount their candlelighting experience. One little boy broke down in tears and poured out the story of the previous night.

Last night, explained Joseph, he proudly arranged the candles in the shiny new menorah and assembled the rest of the family. Unfortunately, he had left his Siddur in school and no matter how hard he tried, he could not remember the brocha. His parents and siblings looked expectantly towards him as his eyes filled with desperate tears. Suddenly, an idea came to him. Shutting his eyes tightly in concentration, he raised the shamas and slowly recited the only words that sprang to mind. "Aleph, bais, gimmel,..." And the family solemnly answered, "Amen!"

These are only a few examples of what Be'er Hagolah accomplishes. Their innovative approach begins with absorption classes for newly-arrived immigrants, featuring English as a second language , Hebrew, and an introduction to the basic concepts of Judaism. Subsequent shabbatonim in areas such as Lakewood, Monsey, Baltimore and Toronto provide wonderful experiences to strengthen their love of Judaism. Perhaps best of all are the Chavrusa and Big Sister programs involving students of Chaim Berlin, Mir, Bais Yaakov and Bnos Leah, to name a few institutions. The programs give the Be'er Hagolah students the chance to form friendships with other Jewish children and provide them with the feeling of acceptance among their peers.

The school often assumes the parental role in placing the students in camps and subsidizing their stay. (Last summer 118 students were placed.) One of the most satisfying tasks the school undertakes is providing financial and emotional support for children who have been accepted into Yeshivos, even purchasing hats, jackets and seforim to complete the needs of these budding *b'nei Torah.*

On the face of things, the success that Be'er Hagolah enjoys seems phenomenal. However, there are thousands of Russian children attending public schools, and countless others, private parochial schools. A most horrifying statistic was brought to light by the founder of St. Sergius Academy. According to Rev. Anthony Grabbe, "a *third* of the students [in his school] are Jewish..."

The faculty of Be'er Hagolah are constantly devising new programs in an attempt to prevent parents from sending their children to these schools, and to attract new students from public schools. As the first day of each school year approaches, the registration roster is checked and rechecked to insure that every student returns and none are lost. A missing name signals panic, along with frantic attempts to reach the child and draw him back.

His name is Mikhail. He was a promising student who dropped out of Be'er Hagolah after eighth grade, much to the dismay of the faculty. His devoted Rebbi maintained contact with him and arranged for a summer job for Mikhail at a religious facility in the country. There he was able to develop friendships with other boys his age. Two years later, Mikhail, now Michoel, is sitting and learning in a well known yeshiva in Boro Park, his love of Torah rekindled by dedicated teacher, good role models, and a large share of siyatah dishmayah.

There are currently almost 600 students studying at Be'er Hagolah. That number is rising dramatically as a result of an estimated 40,000 new Soviet immigrants this year alone. A new state-of-the-art facility is currently under construction in Starret City, Brooklyn, in order to properly provide for the educational, recreational and social needs of the new-comers.

We are privileged to witness a renaissance of Soviet Judaism. As one boy put it, "In Russia there weren't *kippahs* or *tzitzis*, and I wasn't Jewish." Horav Shneur Kotler zt"l said that he became involved in the founding of Be'er Hagolah because someone had to save the children of a tribe that was almost lost to us.

This renewal of interest in Torah Judaism has been long-awaited by the previous generations of Russian Jews, many of whom did not have the opportunity to witness this phenomenon in their own lifetime.

Many years ago in Russia, (where the act of bris milah was illegal), the tzaddik Reb Chaim Zunvel prophesied to a certain Reb Anshel, "Your grandsons will have a bris." At the time, his words were hard to believe, but it came to pass that Reb Anshel's ten and twelve year old grandsons were both zoche to fulfill this obligation upon enrolling in Be'er Hagolah.

The grandfather of another student recounted his father's last wish that no child be named for him unless he had a bris milah. His eyes brimming with tears, the zaideh concluded his words at the bris of his grandson by explaining that the bris held special significance for him, because his grandson Igor, was being renamed Yitzchok, after his great grandfather.

Most of the children choose new Hebrew names from among those of deceased ancestors. But one girl refused to take that course. She insisted on taking her teacher's name as her own (although she was told that this is highly unusual in our circles) because she loved and respected her teacher so much. That student is herself now a teacher at Be'er Hagolah. Recently married to a *ben Torah,* she is now able to reinvest some of the energy and devotion expended upon her by the school administration.

Reb Yaakov Kaminetsky zt"l once said, "Each generation must answer to a different test. Our generation will have to give testimony regarding what we did for Russian Jews."

TABLE OF CONTENTS

Introduction

IT ALL SEEMED TOTALLY ROUTINE. THE TRUCK BEARING THE insignia "Topaz Ironworks" rambled along towards the Swiss-French border on a quiet afternoon in 1942. Loaded inside were the expected boxes of heavy metallic ware. Only a keen-eyed person, noticing the truck's extra-deliberate pace or the special care the driver took when rounding curves, might have suspected that one of the boxes held human cargo.

These were, after all, hardly routine times. The brutal war was providing deadly threats on a daily basis. Countering them often took a great deal of cunning. Smuggling men across the border was far from simple. The three men hidden inside the truck knew that the gamble they were taking was risky. They were all Jewish, and as they were well aware, if caught, their lives would be as good as over. Nazi border patrols were prepared and eager to carry out their duty.

For the men, it was another shared adventure in a friendship that had begun in childhood—the most harrowing one yet. All three had grown up in Austria and had gone to *yeshivah* together. Like most Austrian Jews, they'd considered themselves proud citizens of the motherland. Then the Nazis had marched in, and suddenly they and their fellow Jews had been branded enemies of the state. A desperate flight to Belgium had turned to disaster with their arrest as aliens. Then yet another escape had brought them to France. They'd been safe there, but only briefly, as they watched France, too, fall under Nazi control. Their dashes to freedom seemed to have landed them at a dead end. However, they weren't yet resigned to their doom. One possible plan still gave flight to their hopes. If they could somehow make it across the border to neutral Switzerland they would be beyond the Nazis' clutches.

Despite the danger, they felt they had to make the attempt. There was no other alternative if they wanted to stay free. They'd made contact with someone who had ties to a rescue network. After much planning, he had arranged for them to be smuggled across the border by truck, hidden inside a box.

The conditions inside the crate were hardly comfortable. But as cramped and miserable as they felt, they remained perfectly quiet, especially whenever the truck crawled to a halt. The slightest movement might give them away.

Despite their fears, they encountered no difficulties within the German-occupied French territory. Then the truck arrived at the border itself. A German guard motioned for the driver to make a complete halt.

"Why are you heading to Switzerland?"

"To bring iron equipment there, as you can see."

"What does Switzerland need all this for?"

The driver gave a nonchalant shrug. "I don't ask questions. I just do what they tell me. Can I get going?"

"Not so fast," the German said curtly. "I have to check these boxes out. We've had a lot of smuggling attempts here lately. Things have gotten pretty bloody at times."

"Suit yourself. But they told me to make sure these things were delivered quickly, so I'd appreciate it if you'd hurry it up. I don't want to get fired."

"I couldn't care less about your job," the German said. "I do mine carefully, so don't rush me."

The driver took the guard to the rear of the truck and pointed out the cargo. "There is a lot of stuff back here, and it could take you all day to look through it all. But if you want to take the time, be my guest."

The German surveyed the truck's contents, poking around in a few boxes but skipping over others—including the all-important one. Finally, he was satisfied.

"Everything seems in order," he said. "I just need to check your papers one more time."

"They're in the front."

The driver was about to slam the rear door shut when suddenly the German motioned for him to stop.

"I thought I heard a noise in there."

The men in the box remained deathly still.

The driver gazed into the guard's questioning eyes. Then he abruptly grabbed the cap from his head and whacked it against his side in explosive frustration.

"Did those stupid boxes fall down again?" he thundered. "After all I did to get them just right? I'll bet something inside broke, and I'll bet I get the blame. Just my rotten luck!"

He paused from his tirade long enough to note that the German was still staring at him suspiciously.

"Say," he said to the guard, suddenly sounding chummy, "Would you do me a big favor? Would you help me pile up those boxes in the back again? I'm afraid your uniform might get a little dirty, but with your assistance we can do the job quickly, and I can save a lot of—"

"What!" The German had no patience for this nonsense. "What do you take me for, a servant? Idiot! I'm not helping you with anything! Close this truck up and get it out of my sight before I land you in bigger trouble than your bosses ever will!"

The driver wasted no time in complying. The truck was on Swiss soil within seconds.

Soon, however, the driver reached a well-secluded spot and stopped. He got out, went to the back of the truck and tapped out the prearranged signal. Instantly, the three men materialized—weak, dripping with sweat, but unharmed.

"This is as far as I can take you," the driver told them. "You're on your own now. If you're careful, you should be able to make it. Beware of the local guards, and don't tell anyone where you've come from. I suggest you contact your fellow Jews here as soon as possible. Good luck, and may the Lord help you."

The Jews thanked him warmly for all he'd done and watched as he drove off. Yes, they were indeed on their own now, out of Nazi territory but certainly not out of danger. The Swiss police, they'd been told, were only too happy to cooperate with their German counterparts by turning in aliens. Only Hashem's guidance could bring them to true safety.

As twilight descended, they had no choice but to keep walking. Even though they'd been on their feet all day, a careless stop somewhere might cost them their lives. Tramping on under cover of darkness, they avoided anyone who even vaguely seemed a threat. In time, total exhaustion overcame them. Without food, without water, they could no longer go on.

Suddenly, they spotted a house, its lights still aglow. Should they enter and ask for assistance, or was the possibility of arrest too likely? In the end, their sagging bodies argued decisively for stopping. After praying that they were not about to encounter a trap, the men knocked at the door and waited.

The pipe-smoking, elderly man who opened the door was clearly not a Jew. Still, they proceeded with their presentation.

"We're sorry to bother you at this time of night," they said, "but we're tourists, and we seem to be lost."

The man stared at them intently. "You're not tourists," he finally said. "Not the way you're dressed. You look more like refugees. Am I right?"

The man knew! They felt like making a run for it. But they were too tired to even walk.

"You must be exhausted," the man continued in a softer voice. "Quickly, come inside before anyone sees you. Get a little rest before you continue. You can't stay long, because the border police might find you. But maybe I can help you get on your way."

He escorted them inside and led them to a table. When his wife appeared, he asked her to bring them refreshments. The men quenched their thirst with embarrassed greed.

Finally, one of them could no longer resist asking, "Why are you doing all this for us? You're not Jewish, are you?"

"No," he replied. "But you apparently are. That means we share a common enemy—the cursed Nazis. We Swiss aren't in the war, of course, but that doesn't mean we aren't aware of what's happening around us. We've heard of the atrocities. We've even seen hints of them here when the border police drag refugees away. But our government is acting like a scared rabbit. If our police see Jews sneaking across the border, they're under strict orders to turn them in. Everyone knows that death will follow. We try to delude ourselves. 'It's not our business,' we say. We don't want to make the Germans mad. But we're just as guilty as the Nazis that way, if you ask me. That's why I'm not having any of it. I made a pact with myself. If any refugee comes to me, I help him, no matter what the consequences. I happen to be a policeman myself, but if I'm breaking the law, too bad. That's my way of resisting."

"We're thankful you feel that way," the young Jew responded. "We haven't found too many like you so far."

"What do you think we should do next?" asked one of the

other men. "Is there anywhere we can stay? Any Jews who can shelter us?"

"Not around here. But someone told me that in the city of Montreaux there's a family that helps Jewish refugees. I'll find the name for you. Why don't you go see if they can help you?"

"That won't be easy. We've practically run out of money."

The man considered for a moment. "I'll tell you what. After you rest up a bit, I'll drive you to the train station and get you tickets to Montreaux. And don't worry about the cost. Someday, after the war is over, you'll pay me back."

The man was true to his word. He brought them to the station, hiding them under a blanket in the back seat of his car. After he'd purchased the tickets, he gave them to the men, together with a slip of paper. The single word Sternbuch was written on it.

"That's the family you should contact," he explained. "Ask around when you get to Montreaux, and I'm sure you'll find them. And here's a little pocket money, in case you run into trouble."

They found it hard to express their gratitude. As each of them solemnly shook the man's hand, he nodded. Clearly, he understood what they felt. Then they settled into unobtrusive seats on the train. The journey was, to their relief, uneventful.

During the trip, one of the men remembered that Montreaux was the location of Yeshivas Etz Chaim. Certainly, the *yeshivah* would offer these former *yeshivah* students a hospitable welcome. They could seek refuge there and learn how to contact the Sternbuch family.

Once they reached Montreaux, they ascertained the address of the *yeshivah*. Not knowing how to reach it, the men decided to travel there by taxi. By now it was *Shabbos*, but they knew that if they wandered aimlessly around the streets, they would probably be turned in. It was a matter of life or death. Safety seemed at hand, but who knew for sure?

Thirteen-year-old Avraham Sternbuch walked stiffly along the street as if he were crossing a tightrope. Like any *bar-mitzvah* boy, he was nervous. Yet his edginess was also the product of long-awaited anticipation. His whole family would be present for the ceremony, but the ones he wanted to impress most were his parents Yitzchak and Recha Sternbuch. He'd been looking forward to this chance for a long time now.

Since coming to Montreaux, the Sternbuchs had gained local fame as a model, prosperous Orthodox Jewish family. Mr. and Mrs. Sternbuch ran a successful business, were active in communal affairs and had raised their children in a strictly traditional way. Lately, though, they had been devoting much of their time and energy to a new pursuit: rescuing Jews from the Nazi empire. They would try to arrange for refugees to gain freedom in Switzerland or elsewhere. That often led to their being away from home for lengthy periods of time.

Here, finally, was a chance for Avraham, their oldest son, to do them proud. For a change, the family would be together to share time with each other, and he wanted to bring them much-deserved *nachas*. Avraham had therefore practiced reading his Torah portion until he had it down pat. In only a few minutes, the family would be arriving in *shul*, and the shared *simchah* would begin.

The *bar-mitzvah* would take place in Yeshivas Etz Chaim, where Mrs. Sternbuch's brother-in-law Rabbi Eliyahu Botchko was the *rosh yeshivah*. Accompanying Avraham were his parents, siblings and other relatives.

They had just entered the *yeshivah* when there was a knock at the front entrance. Mrs. Sternbuch opened the door and faced three bedraggled strangers, obviously not dressed for a *bar-mitzvah*.

Most of the family was puzzled, but not Mrs. Sternbuch. Without a word of explanation, she understood.

"Come inside, please," she said, and she shut the door

decisively behind them. "You must have just crossed the border, and you're probably exhausted. Have a seat there, and we'll get you something to eat and drink."

The men began apologizing for having arrived unannounced, and for having come by taxi on *Shabbos*. Mrs. Sternbuch quickly put them at ease.

"Of course, you took a cab," she said. "You had to. Anyone whose life is in danger is allowed to do anything necessary on *Shabbos*. But don't worry anymore. You're with friends now."

Suddenly, another knock reverberated around the room. More refugees? Mrs. Sternbuch hurried back to the door.

"Open up!"

She did. Only this time, the callers were dressed in full uniform. They were accompanied by a taxi driver.

"We're from the Swiss border patrol," their leader said. "We have reason to believe that some illegal refugees have just been brought here by this taxi driver."

Mrs. Sternbuch faced them without flinching. "Well, I'm afraid I don't think I can help you, gentlemen. You see, we're just about to begin services here, and—"

"There they are!" the taxi driver suddenly cried out, pointing to the three men. "Those are the ones I brought here."

Without further ado, the guards stormed into the building and, despite the efforts of the Sternbuchs to dissuade them, took the refugees into custody. The family watched in horror as the three men were led away.

"Where are they taking them?" asked a cousin.

"Straight to the Nazis, I have no doubt," Mrs. Sternbuch said. "We have to save them. And we'd better act immediately."

Then she gazed down at her anxious son and patted his shoulder sympathetically. "I'm so sorry, Avrumy. This is an emergency, as you can see. If we don't do something right away, those men will be doomed. You understand, don't you, dear?"

Avraham frowned a bit, instinctively. Then he nodded firmly, though he knew what would be coming next.

"So you and the rest of the family go on ahead and start *davening*," his mother continued. "Your father and I have to go home for a while. But we'll be back just as soon as all this is taken care of. Don't worry. Everything will go well. We know we can count on you."

"It's okay," Avraham said. "I'll be fine."

"We knew you'd act maturely," his father said. "You've made us really proud."

Avraham managed a smile and watched his parents depart.

As soon as the Sternbuchs were home, they went to work with a will. They began phoning their various contacts in the government, trying to find someone who could provide help. They got nowhere, since all the officials claimed no knowledge of the case.

"You keep phoning," Yitzchak Sternbuch told his wife. "I'll go to police headquarters and see if they have any information."

He rushed over and began peppering the police with questions about the three refugees. At first, they did their best to ignore him, but finally the police captain emerged.

"Oh, yes, those three," he drawled. "They were taken away to a jail in Lausanne."

Mr. Sternbuch thanked him and hurried home.

The next step was summoning contacts in Lausanne and beseeching them to help free the men. One official said he'd investigate. A while later, there was a return call. "There are no Jewish refugees being held here. Someone must have misled you."

The Sternbuchs were furious. Valuable time had been wasted due to the false lead. There was no choice but to start the search over from scratch. Then inspiration struck.

"The police chief in Martiny probably knows where they are," Mrs. Sternbuch said. "He's helped us in the past. It's worth a try."

"But do you know how to reach him?"

"I don't have his private number, but I know someone who does." She mentioned a name. The man lived quite a distance away, and there was another daunting problem, as well.

"He's a *frum* Jew," her husband reminded her. "He'll never answer the phone on *Shabbos*."

"We'll just have to keep trying until he does."

And they did, for twenty long, agonizing minutes. At last, the man answered, figuring it was indeed an emergency. Mrs. Sternbuch explained the desperate situation, and the man willingly supplied the necessary phone number.

When she reached him, the police chief confirmed that he knew the whereabouts of the three refugees.

"I understand your concern for them," he said. "Still, they are in this country illegally. I can't just let them go."

"What if I take full responsibility for them?" Mrs. Sternbuch said. "What if I find a way to make their presence here legal?"

The police chief still expressed reservations, so Mrs. Sternbuch said she would get back to him. Then she immediately got in touch with another of her contacts, Dr. Julius Kuhl, a religious Jew who was the Assistant for Jewish Affairs to Alexander Lados, the Polish Ambassador to Switzerland. Prodded by Mrs. Sternbuch, Dr. Kuhl also called the police chief and told him the refugees would receive Polish protection.

Then, to reinforce his pleas, Dr. Kuhl reached another Sternbuch ally, Monsignor Phillipe Bernardini, the Pope's Ambassador in Switzerland. Bernardini had often championed the Jews' cause in the past, and this case proved no exception. He, too, called the police to express his support for the refugees' release.

A short while later, Monsignor Bernardini phoned the Sternbuchs.

"Good news," he announced succinctly. "They're free."

By this time, the rest of the family had returned from *shul*. Everyone was beaming with admiration over Avraham's outstanding performance. Upon hearing of the three men's release, their spirits soared even higher. Only one person seemed subdued—Avraham himself. Here he'd wanted his parents to share his shining moment with him, and they'd entirely missed it.

Avraham's uncle noticed this. As the rest of the relatives began preparing for the *Shabbos seudah*, he came over to the solemn *bar-mitzvah* boy.

"I understand how you feel," he said. "And I guess anyone in your shoes would feel the same. But maybe you can look at it this way. If not for your *bar-mitzvah* today, your parents might have been away somewhere, and they'd never have met those three men. Then no one would have been able to help them after their arrest. I know you might not see it that way now. But someday you'll realize that your parents have given you the most precious *bar-mitzvah* present in the world. Through you, the lives of three Jews were spared."

A single human life. In light of the enormous world population, it can seem very insignificant indeed.

There is another way to view it, though.

When Elimelech ("Mike") Tress and his associates of Zeirei Agudath Israel began their rescue work in the late 1930s, they ordered stationery for their group. On the bottom of every sheet, they had the following words inscribed: "Whoever saves one life is considered to have saved an entire world."

This quote, derived from a *Mishnah* in *Sanhedrin* (4:5),

provided the driving motivation for Tress and all his rescue colleagues during the Holocaust years. Not all rescue attempts worked out as well as the one that occurred on Avraham Sternbuch's *bar-mitzvah* day. The frustrating failures often outnumbered the gratifying successes. Yet, even when the rescue activists could not save one Jew, they persisted by trying to help another.

Each life, after all, was a precious world in itself. To save a life was to save a world.

Who knew what great contributions that one saved soul might bring to humankind, or how many *mitzvos* he would live to perform? Who could say what supreme heights he and his descendants might rise to? But if a person were allowed to die, then all that potential achievement would be lost forever. As the *Mishnah* points out, Adam was once the solitary inhabitant on earth. Had he perished, human existence would have been doomed. Likewise, if no one saves the life of a unique individual, then who is there to take his place? His passing leaves the world forever at a loss.

Never during their long and often difficult history were so many Jews in greater danger. Never during there long and difficult history were the Jews in greater need of rescue than during the Holocaust.

This volume concentrates on six outstanding Orthodox rescue leaders who performed remarkable feats of *chessed* during and after the Holocaust years. Future volumes will describe the efforts of other outstanding men and women who dedicated themselves to saving and helping their fellow Jews during this tragic time.

The key factor binding all these six heroes and heroines of *hatzalah* was their Torah perspective. They were inspired by the supreme priority placed by the Torah on *areivus* (responsibility), *pidyon shevuyim* (ransoming captives) and *pikuach nefesh* (the overriding importance of saving Jewish lives). These Torah requirements were more important to them than being accepted as equals in non-Jewish society, and therefore, they had no qualms about resorting to such time-honored "Jewish" weapons as bribery, ransom and other illegal means.

The work of these people is not widely known, even in Jewish circles. They were not interested in publicity or honors, only in the success of their mission. Secular historians have mostly ignored them; they either didn't believe, or didn't want to admit, that some "old-fashioned" Orthodox Jews could be so successful in aiding oppressed Jews where so many others had failed. It is time, however, that their stories became general knowledge. Their selfless and courageous efforts should certainly serve as models for Jews of all ages. They are, indeed, heroes of our time.

THE WORKING GROUP
RABBI MICHOEL BER WEISSMANDL

Rabbi Michoel Ber Weissmandl, the "genius of rescue," served as *rosh yeshivah* of an "underground *yeshivah*," while at the same time heading the Jewish underground in Slovakia. He devised many plans for ransoming Jews from the Nazis. He was also the first to warn leaders of world Jewry and the free world of the horrors of Auschwitz, but he was tragically unsuccessful in convincing them to bomb Auschwitz.

1   THE WORKING GROUP

RABBI MICHOEL BER WEISSMANDL

"A MADHOUSE," MURMURED THE YOUNG RABBI. "IT LOOKS LIKE a madhouse." The words echoed over and over in his mind.

He was observing the commotion at the Jews' Center Building in Slovakia, as Jews wailed and pleaded with fellow Jews for their lives on a spring day in 1942.

And as he watched the chaos unfolding before him, the rabbi was filled with anguish and despair. Several weeks earlier, in this very same building, a dramatic meeting had taken place. The Jewish leaders of Slovakia had been summoned by a high official of the pro-Nazi Slovakian government. With him had been a representative of the Nazi leadership itself.

"Listen carefully to the following," the official had said, and he had proceeded to outline the following points:

1. The Jews of Slovakia would soon be resettled in Poland to begin new lives.

2. The younger Jews would be sent first to help pave the way for others to follow.

3. The heads of the Jews' Center would be sent exact

details of the resettlement shortly, and they would be responsible for seeing to it that the Jews carried them out to the letter.

4. Anyone not complying with the above orders would be severely punished.

Once the announcements were over, the official had proclaimed the meeting at an end. Within a few seconds, both he and the Nazi had departed. Also gone was the hope of Slovakia's Jews for a peaceful future.

The first deportations to Poland took place a short while later. On March 26, 1942, a trainload of nine hundred and ninety-nine Jews, mostly young women had been sent to the "labor camps" in the East. Other expulsions followed soon after. Many in the trains believed they were indeed headed for work camps, but most eventually wound up in Auschwitz. Very few would ever return.

By forcing the Jews' Center to play a major role in organizing the deportations, the Nazis were employing their usual devilish cunning. The Jewish leaders knew they either had to persuade their fellow Jews to board the trains or they themselves would be expelled. The deportee, in turn, blamed the Jewish leaders for their plight. Jew had been turned against Jew, to the Nazis' delight. The madness unleashed by the Germans had taken hold.

And so, the Jews' Center Building had become a scene of daily desperation. Jews who had learned that their sons or daughters were to be deported came to plead on their behalf. Their cries and protests pierced the air. And thirty-eight-year-old Rabbi Michoel Ber Weissmandl was a witness to it all.

This scholarly individual, blessed with a sensitive soul and a penetrating mind, had come to the Center to see if he could do anything to aid his fellow Jews. But amidst the pandemonium he encountered, he could accomplish little.

Then a strangely self-satisfied young man, accompanied by a tall Nazi officer, entered the large hall. Rabbi Weissmandl recognized him as Karol Hochberg, a Jewish engineer who had gained virtual political control of the Jews' Center. Rabbi Weissmandl overheard him speaking to the Nazi in a very matter-of-fact tone.

"The last deportation proceeded very smoothly," he reported. "There were exactly three thousand and twenty-eight people sent away, as you ordered."

The Nazi nodded smugly.

Rabbi Weissmandl was dumfounded. Could this be? A Jew discussing his Jewish brothers and sisters as if they were merchandise being efficiently shipped out for sale?

He could take no more and fled the building in utter dismay.

As he roamed the streets numbly, Rabbi Weissmandl noticed a man waving to him. It turned out to be Dr. Ernst Abeles, an old acquaintance and a leader of the Slovakian Jewish community.

"What's wrong?" Dr. Abeles inquired. "You look terrible."

Rabbi Weissmandl described what he had just seen and how horrifying he found Hochberg's conversation with the Nazi.

"That Nazi must have been Dieter Wisliceny," Dr. Abeles noted. "He's Assistant for Jewish affairs to Eichmann, *yemach shemo.*" He was referring to Adolf Eichmann, the supreme implementer of the Nazi scheme to deport and murder the Jews. "The Nazis have apparently sent Wisliceny here to help supervise the deportations. He's supposed to make sure they run smoothly."

"May Hashem curse his efforts," Rabbi Weissmandl muttered.

"But I've heard one interesting bit of news about him. It seems that one Jew who was scheduled to be deported came to him and offered a bribe. Wisliceny took it, and the man was let go."

"Really?" Rabbi Weissmandl considered the implications

of this fact very carefully. "If he let one Jew go, then why not ten? Why not hundreds? If we play our hand right, we might be able to do something about these deportations after all!"

His creative mind was soon a buzz with possible plans. Yet, he quickly realized that success was far from guaranteed. First, he would have to make contact with Wisliceny. But how? Perhaps by reaching him through one of his friends, especially Jewish ones like Hochberg. Much as he abhorred Hochberg and his association with the Nazis, Hochberg might prove a valuable link to Wisliceny. Therefore, Rabbi Weissmandl asked a friend to introduce him to Karol Hochberg.

Hochberg agreed to the encounter but was openly suspicious of Rabbi Weissmandl's motives.

"What do you rabbis want?" he demanded. "Why are you always hounding me? If you ask me, all of you are jealous that I'm so influential in the Jewish community."

Dealing with Hochberg would be difficult and distasteful. But Rabbi Weissmandl had heard that he would be receptive to flattery.

"No, we're not jealous," he replied. "In fact, we're proud that someone of your superior abilities is a leader of our people."

"Oh?" Hochberg asked Rabbi Weissmandl to have a seat. "Now, could you elaborate on that?"

Rabbi Weissmandl proceeded to toss out a few more bland compliments, and Hochberg beamed. Then he told Hochberg that he had come as a representative of fellow rabbis from throughout the world. "We have a very important matter we would like to discuss with your friend Mr. Wisliceny. And we have decided that only someone with outstanding diplomatic and intellectual qualities can bring it to his attention. That is why I've come to you."

"I understand completely," said Hochberg. "What do you have in mind?"

"Let me explain. You see, we feel someone so basically

humane as Wisliceny doesn't really enjoy making Jews suffer. After all, why send them to do labor in Poland when they are needed for tasks right here in Slovakia? So we'd like to ask him to halt the deportations. And we'll make it worth his while if he does so."

"A bribe? Intriguing. But how do you plan to get the money for that?"

"Don't worry," Rabbi Weissmandl said. "We have plenty of connections, so it won't be a problem. The point is, we need someone with close ties to Wisliceny to bring all this to his attention. And we think no one would be better for this all-important mission than you."

Hochberg considered the offer. "This might be dangerous. What if he gets upset? These Nazis are hard to predict. Why should I put my high position on the line?"

"Think of it this way," Rabbi Weissmandl replied. "The Germans may lose the war. If they do, someone might accuse you of having helped them, and that can lead to trouble. But if you help us in this matter, we can testify that you were a true humanitarian, and you'll get off. Besides, we might be able to show you our appreciation in . . . tangible ways, if it all works out."

Hochberg thought it over and then nodded decisively. "All right, I'll meet with Wisliceny. For the sake of my fellow Jews."

Hochberg made an appointment to see the Nazi. Before the designated time, Rabbi Weissmandl coached him intensively on what to tell Wisliceny and what to avoid saying. Then, on the appointed day, came the wait, the long, agonizing wait. If Hochberg failed, they might be in even bigger trouble than before. But if he succeeded . . .

Finally, Hochberg returned. To Rabbi Weissmandl's great relief, he was in high spirits.

"My friend Wisliceny thought very highly of the plan," he reported. "He says he wants fifty thousand American dollars in order to carry it out."

Fifty thousand American dollars—a fortune! Who had that sort of money when even in America they earned only twenty-five dollars a week? And the government had made it illegal to own American currency. Yet, Rabbi Weissmandl would not let these factors deter him.

"And if we do get him the money?" he asked Hochberg.

"Then the deportations will stop."

Rabbi Weissmandl smiled and silently prayed.

Raising the funds to pay Wisliceny did indeed turn out to be a most difficult task, as will be explained later. But they were eventually found, and Wisliceny was true to his word.

The deportations ceased.

For over fifty thousand Slovakian Jews, this development had come too late; they had already been taken away. But for about two years after Wisliceny's order, the remaining twenty-five thousand Jews in Slovakia were safe. They could live without the terror of being forced from their homes and sent to unknown destinations. During that time, some managed to escape to other countries. Had the deal with Wisliceny not been made, they too would have been doomed.

For Rabbi Michoel Ber Weissmandl, it would not be the last of his valiant efforts to extract Jews from the Nazis' grip. Yet it would remain a highlight in a life devoted to saving and serving his fellow Jews.

A YOUTHFUL PRODIGY

That life began on the 4th of Marcheshvan, 5664 (1904), in the city of Debrecen, Hungary. When Michoel was still young, his family moved to the town of Tirnau in Czechoslovakia, where his father served as a *shochet*. Reb Yosef Weissmandl was a pious man who was especially mindful of the power of *tefillos*. At night, he used to check to see that his children were sleeping soundly and pray they would grow up to be wise and caring Jews. Hashem more than granted his wish.

Michoel began his Torah studies in the local *cheder* and then learned in the *yeshivah* of Rabbi Dovid Wesserly in the nearby city of Sered. His breathtaking ability to analyze the holy texts was already evident when he was still very young.

As his *bar-mitzvah* approached, Michoel composed a long and brilliant *drashah* to be delivered on this important occasion. Among the guests who arrived for the celebration was his grandfather Reb Menachem Meir Berthauer. Michoel mentioned that he was looking forward to delivering the *drashah* after he had worked so hard to prepare it.

His grandfather asked to see the speech. After reading it through, he told the boy, "Michoel, this is remarkable, especially since you wrote it yourself. But I will give you ten gold crowns if you do *not* read it at the *bar-mitzvah*."

Michoel was stunned. "Why? Is it full of mistakes?"

"On the contrary. Everything in it seems wonderfully thought out and perfectly correct. But I am afraid that, if you deliver this *drashah*, everyone will praise you so highly that you'll get a swelled head. And you know that arrogance is not a proper trait for a Jew."

Michoel looked at the speech on which he had labored for so long and with so much effort. Then he folded it up and put it away. He would listen to his grandfather. At the *bar-mitzvah* he delivered a short, simple *Dvar Torah* instead. His grandfather gave him the ten gold crowns as promised, and with the money Michoel bought a copy of Rabbeinu Bachya's commentary on the Torah.

As it turned out, Rabbi Weissmandl did use the drashah, but only thirty-six years later, when he was a *rosh yeshivah* in America. His students, young men in their twenties, gathered around as he lectured to them for over an hour. When he finished, they expressed their admiration for the insights they had just heard. It was then that Rabbi Weissmandl shyly remarked, "Incidentally, that was the *bar-mitzvah drashah* my grandfather persuaded me not to use."

A NEW TORAH MASTER

As a young man, Rabbi Weissmandl continued his learning under Rabbi Shmuel Dovid Ungar, with whom he established a uniquely strong bond. Not only did he emerge as a teacher in Rabbi Ungar's *yeshivah*, but in 1937, he also became Rabbi Ungar's son-in-law, marrying his daughter Bracha Rachel. Earlier, when Rabbi Ungar had been invited to become the *rav* of the city of Nitra, Rabbi Weissmandl had urged him to stay in Tirnau. But Rabbi Ungar had accepted the assignment, explaining that he had the feeling that a *yeshivah* in Nitra would one day outlast all other European *yeshivos*. And, in fact, the Nitra Yeshivah remained open until nearly the end of the war, long after the Nazis had closed down all other Eastern European *yeshivos*. When Rabbi Ungar went to Nitra, Rabbi Weissmandl came with him.

Rabbi Weissmandl became Rabbi Ungar's chief assistant at the Nitra Yeshivah, serving as both an administrator and a *rebbe*. He also continued his studies and journeyed throughout Poland and Lithuania to visit such Torah luminaries as the Chofetz Chaim, the Gerrer Rebbe, Rabbi Chaim Ozer Grodzensky and Rabbi Elchonon Wasserman. Rabbi Weissmandl also traveled several times to Oxford, England, in order to examine rare Hebrew manuscripts in the library there. In England, Rabbi Weissmandl also established a warm friendship with Rabbi Solomon Schonfeld, a young British Torah educator who had been his *talmid* in Nitra. The two kept up a close correspondence, and using Rabbi Weissmandl as his role model, Rabbi Schonfeld would also become a leading rescue leader.

Once, an ancient manuscript was added to the library

collection, and no one on the staff could identify its authorship. When Rabbi Weissmandl, using his scholarly knowledge, provided the writer's name, the grateful librarian let him use the library whenever he wished. His research there enabled him to prepare new editions of classic *sefarim*, complete with notes based on the manuscripts he had found.

It was in England that Rabbi Weissmandl achieved his first success in *hatzalah* (rescue) work.

INTRODUCTION TO HATZALAH

It took place in the spring of 1938, before the war in Europe began. Germany had annexed Austria, and Hitler ordered the expulsion of Jews from the province of Burgenland. After all their money and possessions had been confiscated, they were sent to Vienna, where they arrived penniless. Rabbi Weissmandl rushed to Vienna to meet with their leaders and try to help.

Then the Nazis put sixty rabbis, mostly from Burgenland, on a ship bound for nowhere. In effect, they were announcing, "We don't want these Jews. Let's see if anyone else does."

The ship appealed to Czechoslovakia but was refused admittance there. Then the rabbis thought of going on to Austria, but the Austrian authorities wired back a message: "No entry." Other countries gave the same uncaring response. What to do next?

Rabbi Weissmandl flew to England. Using the connections he and his colleague Rabbi Solomon Schonfeld had developed there, he secured an appointment with the Archbishop of Canterbury, the head of the Anglican (English) Church.

"Sir," Rabbi Weissmandl said forthrightly. "I know that, as a religious man, you have great respect for human life. There are sixty holy rabbis now stranded on a ship somewhere in Europe. No country is willing to give them refuge. If they don't reach safety soon, the Nazis will no doubt take them back into custody—and probably put them to death. Can you use your good offices to help them?"

Moved by his sincere plea, the Archbishop contacted the British Foreign Office, which was in charge of immigration. The response came quickly: England granted entry visas to the sixty rabbis, and they were saved.

Success, however, would not always be so forthcoming. In November, 1938, hoping to avoid war, the heads of England and France met with Hitler at Munich. They agreed to his demands to take over parts of Czechoslovakia, which was soon carved up. One area became the independent country of Slovakia, which was soon led by a pro-Nazi government. Another part was taken over by Hungary. Many Jews lived in this annexed area, and Hungary ordered their immediate expulsion.

Once again, Rabbi Weissmandl got in touch with the Archbishop of Canterbury and asked him to intercede with the British authorities on the Jews' behalf. The Archbishop passed along the urgent plea.

This time, though, the British did nothing. They claimed the Jews were not guaranteed protection under the provisions of the Munich agreements.

THE WORKING GROUP

Once the war was under way, Rabbi Weissmandl remained based in Slovakia. During the week, he stayed in the city of Pressburg, where he conducted his rescue work. For *Shabbos*, though, he returned to Nitra, some forty miles away. There he learned and taught at the *yeshivah* and enjoyed the *Shabbos seudos* with his growing family.

RABBI MICHOEL BER WEISSMANDL

In Pressburg, he helped organize a Jewish underground movement to save Jews from the Nazis. Its purpose was to protect and assist Slovakian Jewry and to thwart Nazi measures against them wherever possible. Among its numerous projects were securing kosher food for Jews sent to labor camps and aiding in the rescue of Jewish refugees. The committee was called, simply, the Working Group, and its membership included Mrs. Gisi Fleischmann (a cousin of Rabbi Weissmandl and a true woman of valor), Rabbi Armin Frieder and Andre Steiner.

In February, 1942, when the Slovakian government under pro-Nazi president Joseph Tiso issued a decree that all Jews between the ages of fifteen and forty-five had to register with the police, Rabbi Weissmandl urged his fellow Jews not to comply. He reasoned (correctly, as it turned out) that the Nazis would later use the list of registered Jews for purposes of expulsion. He also strongly advised Jews to prepare bunkers and other hiding places for use in case the situation deteriorated.

It soon did. The deportations of Jews from Slovakia began the very next month. Once they started, they continued relentlessly.

By the time Rabbi Weissmandl successfully used the time-tested method of bribing Dieter Wisliceny to stop the expulsions, as described at the beginning of this chapter, over two-thirds of Slovakia's Jews had already been taken away.

THE RESCUER WHO DIDN'T EXIST

The approach to Wisliceny required careful preparation. Rabbi Weissmandl surmised that if just anyone offered the Nazi a bribe, it would have a limited effect at best. Wisliceny would accept it that once and then might resume the deportations soon after. However, if Wisliceny thought that the bribe was coming from a representative of wealthy American Jews, he might be eager to make further deals in the future, in the hope of gaining greater riches. Wisliceny, he had learned, was a staunch believer in the Nazi propaganda that rich, powerful Jews controlled the United States. As a result, the Nazi wanted to make contact with well-to-do American Jews. He not only wanted to gain access to their wealth, but he had begun thinking that, if he made deals with them, they might defend him if Germany lost the war. He also hoped that these influential Jews would pressure their government to side with Germany against what he considered their common enemy—Russia.

Rabbi Weissmandl decided to take advantage of these delusions. He had always had a creative mind. In England he had created a mechanical object that had so impressed the British, they had asked him to remain there. And so now, for rescue purposes, he invented a man who didn't even exist.

The "man's" name was Ferdinand Roth. Rabbi Weissmandl fabricated his identity out of thin air. He created "Roth" as a resident of Switzerland who had been appointed as a proxy of rich American Jews. Thus, when Rabbi Weissmandl sent Karol Hochberg to meet with Wisliceny to discuss an end to the deportations, he told Hochberg he would be acting as an agent of "Ferdinand Roth." Hochberg, of course, never met Roth, but he thought he was an actual person. To deceive him and others, Rabbi Weissmandl presented letters from Roth. In reality, these were elegantly-written letters typed by Rabbi Weissmandl himself, using a fancy borrowed typewriter, on stationery obtained from a first-class Swiss hotel.

Wisliceny was also fooled. In fact, he was so impressed with the stylish writing in the letters he presumed that only a well-heeled person could have produced them. As a result, he was willing to conduct protracted negotiations with representatives of Roth and agreed to halt the deportations upon receiving fifty thousand American dollars.

Wisliceny's terms were clear. He said he would immediately cancel the next three transports of Jews, as a sign of good will. However, within ten days of this friendly act, he wanted the first part of the Jews' payment–twenty-five thousand American dollars. If that amount was produced on time, there would be no further transports for the next seven weeks. At the end of this period, the remaining twenty-five thousand dollars would be due. Once that arrived, the deportations would remain suspended indefinitely.

TWO DOLLARS A JEW

Rabbi Weissmandl was overjoyed. For a few thousand dollars, the lives of some twenty-five thousand Slovakian Jews would be spared. It came out to just two dollars per Jew. Raising the funds couldn't prove to be too herculean a task.

Or could it?

He quickly organized a committee to acquire the funds and suggested it be headed by Mrs. Gisi Fleischmann. Mrs. Fleischmann was the daughter of Rabbi Yehudah Fischer, who was Rabbi Weissmandl's great-uncle. She also had close ties with Slovakia's secular Jewish leaders. Throughout the next few years, she was to prove herself a heroic rescue activist many times over.

The committee's members reluctantly agreed to work with Karol Hochberg, despite their intense personal dislike of him, because of his friendly relations with Wisliceny.

Then word came that Wisliceny had indeed stopped the scheduled deportations, as promised. Now it was up to the Working Group to find the money.

However, this was complicated by the fact that anti-Jewish laws had reduced most of the remaining Slovakian Jews to poverty. Jews were no longer allowed to work as doctors, lawyers or pharmacists, and Jewish-owned factories had been turned over to non-Jews. Furthermore, the money to be paid to Wisliceny had to be exclusively in American dollars, and the process of obtaining funds from abroad was also very difficult. World War II had already begun, and the Allies had banned the sending of money to Nazi-controlled countries.

The ten-day deadline was drawing near.

Quickly, Rabbi Weissmandl made contact with his friend Benjamin Shloime Stern, a businessman and currency dealer who was a Jewish community leader in Pressburg. Mr. Stern coaxed his friends into donating much of the money. When that amount still fell short of the required total, Stern told Rabbi Weissmandl, "I will give you the rest of the money myself."

"But you couldn't possibly have that much cash in your possession," Rabbi Weissmandl said. "The authorities have been confiscating Jewish property right and left. They wouldn't have let you keep thousands of dollars."

"Come and see."

Stern brought Rabbi Weissmandl to the garden behind his home. Suddenly, he began shoveling the earth, and soon some American currency became visible in the soil. As he dug further, more and more bills emerged, until finally all the necessary money had been obtained.

"I was keeping it hidden there in case of an emergency," Stern explained, "and this is certainly an emergency. But of course, you can't give Wisliceny money that smells like rotten vegetables."

All that night, therefore, he and his wife cleaned the bills and even ironed them. The next day, the money, looking crisp and fresh, was delivered to Wisliceny. The Nazi accepted it with glee.

"Good. I see you've collected the money. And all in new American bills, too. So the American Jews can really produce cash when they want to. Now I'll keep my part of the bargain.

I'll order the deportations suspended for the time being. But don't forget. The next payment is due in seven weeks, on August 13. Make sure it arrives on time, or else you will deeply regret it."

THE SEARCH FOR THE MISSING FUNDS

As the Jews of Slovakia breathed more easily, the Working Group began seeking the remaining twenty-five thousand dollars.

Mr. Stern had been most generous, but he and his friends had already exhausted the extent of their assets. It was time to turn to some of the wealthy Jewish organizations in the free world. Orthodox Jewish rescue groups like the Vaad Hatzalah had only recently been formed, and were therefore in no position to contribute the huge sums of money required. Surely, thought Rabbi Weissmandl, these renowned groups could tap their considerable financial resources and come to the aid of Slovakia's Jews. Messengers were sent to their offices with urgent appeals for help.

Their reply, in effect, was as follows: "We understand your plight, and we'd like to help. But there's a war on, and we will not conduct any deals with the Nazis or their allies. It's immoral and illegal, and will make us seem unloyal to the Allies' cause. Therefore, we have no choice but to say no."

The members of the Working Group were stunned.

"They don't understand!" Rabbi Weissmandl complained. "This is an emergency! Lives are hanging in the balance! This isn't the time to quibble about technicalities."

He refused to submit to despair and stepped up his campaign. The Working Group wrote increasingly urgent letters to the various Jewish organizations, pleading for funds. The deadline set by Wisliceny was rapidly approaching. If the money were not raised, the deportations would resume.

One of the first persons the Working Group turned to was Mr. Saly Mayer. Mayer was the most influential Jew in Switzerland at that time. Would he use his high position for the benefit of Slovakia's imperiled Jews?

Mayer's reply soon arrived, containing the following points:

1. Slovakia was just a small territory, with only a few thousand Jews. Therefore, the princely sum of twenty-five thousand dollars was far too much to allocate on their behalf.

2. Furthermore, the Working Group members were probably exaggerating the seriousness of the situation, since Eastern European Jews tended to make matters sound worse than they were.

3. In any case, there was no chance of sending even a token sum now, since the money would have to come from America, and American law forbade sending funds to an enemy country.

4. At best, some maintenance money could be sent on a monthly basis, as before, from funds left over in Hungary.

Case closed.

Another Jewish communal leader, Nathan Schwalbe of the Hechalutz, a Slovakian Socialist Zionist movement, told the group that the main goal of Jews should be to establish a Jewish State after the war. In order to gain this, the Jews would have to win the world's sympathy by suffering during the war. "Only by making sacrifices will we have a state," he declared, and the sacrifice would be made by European Jews facing the Nazis' guns.

All the participants of the Working Group, including the Zionist members, were dumfounded by these insensitive replies. They could not believe these Jewish leaders were giving precedence to other considerations before their brothers' welfare.

THE NAZIS GROW IMPATIENT

The August 13 deadline loomed before them.

Rabbi Weissmandl knew that drastic action was needed. He wrote a letter on Swiss hotel stationery in the name of Ferdinand Roth, stating that the messenger who was supposed to have brought the money to Wisliceny had broken his leg and was in the hospital. There would be a short delay until the messenger recovered.

Rabbi Weissmandl then paid someone to smuggle the letter to Switzerland and mail it, creating the impression that it had indeed emanated from there. The missive was addressed to Karol Hochberg, who delivered it to Wisliceny. The Nazi agreed to hold off on further deportations. For now.

As the last days of August dashed by, the Working Group scrambled furiously for funds. They continued sending feverish pleas to Jews around the world, and kept getting rejections.

Wisliceny called in Hochberg. It was not a pleasant meeting. The Nazi was losing his patience.

In desperation, Rabbi Weissmandl dispatched yet another letter from Ferdinand Roth, explaining that the messenger's recuperation was taking longer than expected. The payment would therefore be further delayed. He then waited and hoped, as *Rosh Hashanah* approached.

Still no money.

Finally, Wisliceny's tolerance expired.

"Enough!" he told his aides just before *Shabbos Shuvah*. "Those Jews are just stalling. It's time to show them we mean business."

"And how would you suggest proving that, sir?"

"I want three thousand Slovakian Jews put on a train and sent to Auschwitz."

The Working Group's worst fears had been realized.

Rabbi Weissmandl sent out last-ditch letters to Jewish leaders in Hungary, warning that the lives of their Slovakian brothers and sisters were in the greatest jeopardy. Money had to be sent *immediately*, even if it meant desecrating *Shabbos* or *Yom Tov* to do so.

On the eve of *Yom Kippur* itself, while the rest of the Jews of Nitra were on their way to *shul*, Rabbi Weissmandl was in the local post office. He was sending cables to three Orthodox Jewish leaders of Budapest, Hungary, in the name of his father-in-law Rabbi Ungar. Rabbi Weissmandl knew that even Orthodox leaders were reluctant to send the money. Possessing American dollars was illegal in Hungary. Heeding his request might cause major problems. Nevertheless, he kept after them. For after all, if Orthodox Jews didn't rally behind the ideals of *hatzalas nefashos* and *pidyon shvuyim*, then who would?

Therefore, he wired them this blunt message: "I hereby summon you tomorrow, on *Yom Kippur*, to appear before the Heavenly Court and answer the charge that you are guilty of not coming to the aid of the holy Jews of Slovakia!"

A RESPONSE . . . TOO LATE

The pressure finally bore fruit. On the day after *Yom Kippur*, an Orthodox Jewish community leader from Hungary at last arrived with the long-sought twenty-five thousand dollars. Rabbi Weissmandl rushed the sum to Karol Hochberg, who brought it to Wisliceny. As Rabbi Weissmandl had requested, Hochberg asked that Wisliceny bring back the transport of Jews sent out a few days before.

"Sorry," scowled Wisliceny. "They're already gone. They can't return. And let that be a lesson to you Jews. Next time, don't hold back on the payments. You keep your part of the bargain, and I'll keep mine."

For three thousand Jews on their way to Auschwitz, the delay had proved tragically fateful. But for the remaining Jews of Slovakia, there now began a two-year period of relative calm. Additional bribes guaranteed Wisliceny's cooperation in keeping the transports suspended. When Slovakian officials urged him to start sending Jews to Auschwitz again and thereby please Hitler, he refused. "Until I finish examining their papers," Wisliceny said, "the Jews must stay where they are." And that examination kept dragging on and on . . .

The success of this venture gave the Working Group great encouragement. It prompted Rabbi Weissmandl to broaden the scope of the group's activities, and he pressed his colleagues to think big. After all, if the Jews of Slovakia could be ransomed, then why couldn't the same be done for the other remaining Jews of Nazi-controlled Europe?

He was referring to the hundreds of thousands of Jews still under the Nazis' thumb in Poland, France, Greece, Holland, Rumania and other countries. The Nazis still stood unopposed in these areas, but they were beginning to suffer battlefield defeats elsewhere throughout the world. Maybe the realization that they might yet lose the war would put them in a mood to negotiate for Jewish lives.

THE BOLD EUROPA PLAN

Rabbi Weissmandl therefore came up with the most ambitious rescue scheme devised during the war. It was called the Europa Plan, and it aimed at nothing less than securing the freedom of all Europe's remaining Jews through a huge bribe to the Nazis.

The Nazis' initial reaction to the plan was promising. In the fall of 1942, Karol Hochberg brought a proposal from Ferdinand Roth to Wisliceny, outlining the Europa Plan. Wisliceny reacted favorably. Believing the proposal had come from the powerful leaders of world Jewry, he was pleased. "Maybe these Jews will use their vast connections to come to terms with us and join us in our struggle against Russia instead."

A few days later, he told Hochberg that high-ranking Nazi leaders had also expressed interest in the plan. "Once you put some money on the table, we can start talking business."

Once again, the Working Group scrounged around the world via letters and telegrams for money. It would be easier this time, they reasoned. After all, hadn't bribe money already halted the Slovakian deportations? And didn't this prove beyond a doubt the effectiveness of negotiating with the Nazis to save lives?

Not necessarily. Again, Saly Mayer and other representatives of Jewish groups raised stern objections. Bribery was against the law and also degrading, they asserted.

"I don't understand how these people can eat and sleep and go about their daily lives as if everything were normal," Rabbi Weissmandl wondered aloud. "Here we've been crying to them for help for months on end, and they've done almost nothing."

As the search for money continued, so did the negotiations with Wisliceny. Karol Hochberg was no longer involved. He had been arrested by the government on charges of intrigue and sentenced to a two-year jail term. After his release, he joined the anti-Nazi partisans but was assassinated by one of the group on suspicion of having collaborated with the Germans.

A SPELLBINDING PERSONALITY

Taking Hochberg's place in the Wisliceny negotiations was Andre Steiner, an architect by trade and a member of the Working Group. Steiner was a secular Jew without any ties to religion. Nevertheless, when he first met Rabbi Weissmandl, he found himself drawn to the latter's fascinating personality and saintly ways. Steiner was amazed that this scholarly man could be so bubbling with charisma and good humor, and he admired his intuitive way of sizing up and dealing with his fellow man. Thus, when Rabbi Weissmandl, early in their relationship, asked Steiner to provide kosher food for a group of Jews, this irreligious Jew who had never eaten kosher in his life felt compelled to comply immediately.

Before every meeting with Wisliceny, Steiner received intensive coaching from Rabbi Weissmandl. "First Wisliceny will say this, and you will say the following," the rabbi instructed. And to Steiner's amazement, that was exactly how the discussions later proceeded.

As Steiner left for his first encounter with the Nazi, Rabbi Weissmandl shook his hand. "May the Almighty grant you success on your holy mission," he said warmly.

Steiner suddenly felt supremely confident that no harm would befall him on the trip, as if Rabbi Weissmandl's blessing had given him Divine protection.

CONFRONTATION

In fact, Wisliceny gave Steiner anything but a hearty welcome. The moment the Nazi set eyes upon Steiner, he began hurling a torrent of curses and accusations at him. He charged the Jews with a wide variety of crimes and ranted that if they didn't soon change their ways, they would be doomed.

Steiner's face reddened as he listened to this crazed diatribe. Finally, he could take no more, and with impetuous courage, he answered: "You believe Germany will win the war, don't you? Well, we think you may in the end lose. And if that happens, and people see how you've oppressed the Jews and sent them to death camps, then where will you be?"

Wisliceny stared at him furiously.

"On the other hand," Steiner went on, "if you continue to help us in exchange for money, then we have reason to show our gratitude. For instance, we can testify that you should be given leniency because you saved many lives. But let me assure you, Herr Wisliceny, that if you shout insults, we'll have nothing good to say about you at all, and you'll get what's coming to you."

Wisliceny listened to this outburst in silence. When it was over, he blushed. Then he turned to Steiner and said in a quiet voice, "Have a seat, Herr Steiner."

From then on, he treated Steiner with the utmost courtesy.

Eventually, Wisliceny came up with concrete proposals. In exchange for two million American dollars, the Germans would stop *all* expulsions everywhere, except for Poland. After a first payment of two hundred thousand dollars, the expulsions would be stopped for two months. Then the next payment would be due. Wisliceny indicated he was making this offer with the approval of very high-ranking Nazis.

DO OR DIE

The Working Group now had a clear-cut, overriding goal to reach. Mrs. Gisi Fleischmann was dispatched to Hungary to raise funds and was received politely by the Jewish leaders there. But because the Jews in Hungary were still relatively untouched by the havoc of war, they couldn't appreciate the true seriousness of the situation. Mrs. Fleischmann returned from her mission sorely disappointed, the recipient of good wishes but hardly any money.

Writing furiously, Rabbi Weissmandl kept firing off one letter after another, extending pleas to anyone who might respond. He kept reminding everyone that, whereas breaking a man-made law was regrettable, not saving the lives of fellow Jews would violate Hashem's commands. And he warned that if they did not grab at this unexpected opportunity another chance might never come, and the worst bloodbath in Jewish history would ensue.

The letters, powerful as they were, had only a minor effect. Some of the secular Jewish groups could not find it within themselves to place their faith in an Orthodox rabbi. As a result, they discounted his sense of urgency.

Saly Mayer, under pressure, finally agreed to raise the two hundred thousand dollars. However, he would not give it to the Germans outright. Instead, he would only agree to put the money in an American bank, where the Nazis would be able to obtain it—after the war.

The Nazis were no fools. They put no stock in an unpredictable future; they wanted the money right away. As Rabbi Weissmandl had warned, they quickly turned this idea down flat.

In September 1943, the negotiations between the Germans and the Working Group broke down. The Germans were demanding payment, and the Jews had no large sums of money to offer. Only in 1944, when the Nazis were already rushing trainloads of Hungarian Jews to Auschwitz, were they willing to resume the talks. By then, though, the Germans' conditions had stiffened. No longer would they agree to release *all* the remaining European Jews (of whom there were now far fewer). Instead, they would only free select groups of Jews. And they demanded a far higher payment than before.

The question still bothers many historians: Would the Nazis have kept their word? Would they actually have released so many Jews after receiving the payment, or would they have just kept the money and continued the killing anyway?

No one can say for sure. Nevertheless, there is some evidence that the Nazis were indeed preparing to carry out the agreement. Two Jews who escaped from the Auschwitz-

Birkenau death camp reported that in July, 1943, while the negotiations were under way, transports of Jews to the camp had suddenly ceased for a while. Even the gas chambers had lain idle during this interval.

In addition, a special transport of Jews from Thereisienstadt had come to Auschwitz, and for six months they had been treated by the Nazis with unheard-of respect. Perhaps these Jews were being prepared for release as part of the deal. When the negotiations foundered, though, these Jews were also sent to their deaths.

Rabbi Weissmandl had no doubts that a tremendous opportunity to rescue Jews had been lost and that the Europa Plan had never really been put to the test. To the end of his life, he was bitter in his denunciations of Jewish leaders who, he felt, could have rescued so many but who had not been daring enough to try. In his view, they never even gave the plan a chance.

As matters developed, Rabbi Weissmandl's scheme did play a role in later rescue attempts, some of which proved to be at least partially successful.

After the Nazis took control of Hungary in 1944, Jewish negotiations with the Nazis were taken over by two Hungarian Zionist leaders, Joel Brand and Rudolf Kastner, who nudged the Orthodox group (led by Phillip Freudinger) out of the picture. Brand and Kastner based their proposals on Rabbi Weissmandl's bold Europa Plan, and the infamous Nazi Adolf Eichmann himself offered them a deal–Jewish lives in exchange for trucks and other goods. Brand was sent to the Middle East to meet with Zionist leaders and gain their approval for the trade. However, once there he was arrested by the British and taken into custody. With this, the plan came to nought.

However, back in Hungary, Kastner managed to get a trainload of Jews released from Nazi control in exchange for bribe money. Yitzchok and Recha Sternbuch, Orthodox Jewish rescue leaders in Switzerland, were instrumental in channelling funds from the New York-based Vaad Hatzalah for this venture. At a critical juncture in these talks, when Eichmann was demanding proof that the Jews would provide the trucks, a letter from Ferdinand Roth arrived. Written in Rabbi Weissmandl's elegant style, it assured the Nazis that several hundred tractors were being purchased in Switzerland to meet their terms. The letter helped keep the talks from collapsing.

In the end, almost seventeen hundred Jews from the train were allowed, in stages, to reach Switzerland and freedom. Furthermore, the Nazis kept some eighteen thousand other Jews in Austria in reserve as pawns in case any similar trades might occur. None ever did, but these Jews managed to survive the war anyway.

TAKING RISKS

Meanwhile, throughout 1943 and 1944, the Jews of Slovakia remained in a state of suspended apprehension. The Nazis were leaving them alone, but the Jews knew that the status quo could change at a moment's notice. To keep the pressure off, the Working Group continued bribing Wisliceny and Slovakian officials. In addition, they helped maintain Jewish labor camps in Slovakian cities like Sered and Novaky. The government had set up these camps for Jews who had been forced to resign their jobs. The Working Group paid dearly to ensure that the workers received decent treatment there, and Rabbi Weissmandl saw to it that kosher kitchens were set up in the camps. The Working Group's hope was that if the government and Slovakian public saw that the Jews were leading productive lives in the camps they would be in no rush to deport them. For two years, that remained the case.

However, thousands of Slovakian Jews had been expelled to Poland at the beginning of the war, and Rabbi

Weissmandl maintained contact with as many of these exiles as he could. To ease their plight, the Working Group smuggled in money, food and clothing for their benefit. When possible, they helped arrange for these Jews and their Polish counterparts to be spirited across the border to Slovakia or Hungary.

Such activities were, of course, illegal and perilous. The Working Group members were always at risk, and Rabbi Weissmandl himself was arrested by the authorities. During harsh and lengthy interrogation, he protested that he had only been trying to help his fellow Jews lead normal lives.

"What is illegal about trying to make sure they can eat a decent meal and wear decent clothing?" he asked.

Finally, his captors agreed, and he was released. For a while, the Group was given permission to send parcels to Jews in Poland without further interference.

By 1944, the war picture looked distinctly brighter. The Russians had routed the Nazis at Stalingrad, and the Americans and British were about to open a Western front at Normandy. If only the remaining Jews of Hungary and Slovakia could hold out a while longer, until an Allied victory, perhaps they would survive the war in relatively large numbers. Sadly, it was not to be so.

HORROR OVERTAKES HUNGARY

In early 1944, the Germans grew increasingly suspicious that the leaders of Hungary were trying to negotiate a separate peace with the Allies. As a result, on March 19, 1944, the still potent German army marched into Hungary and occupied the country. The Jews of Hungary were about to face their darkest hour.

The previous government of Admiral Horthy, although it had passed many anti-Jewish laws and consigned Jewish men to labor battalions, had been relatively benign when compared to the Nazis. Under the Nazis, Horthy was allowed to remain as the nominal leader. However, the Germans retained ultimate control and now unleashed their barbarity. The Jews of Hungary were ordered to wear the Star of David, they were prohibited from traveling on trains, and they had to give up their cars, radios and even telephones. But that was only the beginning.

Adolf Eichmann and his aides descended upon Hungary like a pack of bloodthirsty wolves to apply the Final Solution to this hitherto untouched territory. They were by now masters of the art of mass murder, and they quickly introduced Hungarian Jewry to their monstrously efficient methods.

The first step, as elsewhere, was to concentrate the Jews into ghettos. Then, on April 24, 1942, the first Hungarian Jews were deported from these ghettos to Auschwitz. On May 15, mass expulsions began, at the rate of twelve thousand Jews per day. By June 20, over four hundred thousand Hungarian Jews had been carted off to the death camps. At this point, those in Budapest remained the only large-scale Jewish community in Hungary.

CONFIRMING THE UNBELIEVABLE

To Rabbi Weissmandl and the others in the Working Group, this was a shattering blow. By now, they knew exactly what lay in store for the Hungarian Jews.

The fact that Jews were being killed *en masse* was, by 1944, common knowledge to the Group. As early as 1942, while coming to the aid of Slovakian Jews exiled to Poland, Rabbi Weissmandl had been severely unnerved by a message smuggled out of Poland. It had come from a Polish Jew about to be sent to Auschwitz. Written in a shaky hand on a piece of crumpled paper, it read, "Help us, brothers, in the Name of

Heaven! We are all about to be murdered!" Subsequent reports had confirmed this awful prediction.

The Working Group members were therefore under no false illusions about the Hungarian Jews' eventual fate. Even then, though, they didn't realize the full scope of the Nazis' unimaginable brutality. Only in 1944 did this become clear to them in all its stark detail.

That year, two Jewish concentration camp inmates, Walter Rosenberg (Rudolph Vrba) and Alfred Wetzler (Josef Lanik), managed the daring escape from Auschwitz. They made their way to Slovakia and met there with members of the Working Group. Being among the very first to supply a first-hand report to the ouside world of the horrors of Auschwitz, they were rare eyewitnesses to crimes beyond belief. Yet, because they had been there, their word could not be denied. Rabbi Weissmandl listened to their account of the daily tragedies with mounting shock. When they finished, he broke down in wracking sobs. He may not have known the victims personally, but to him they were all members of his family. He grieved bitterly at his inability to save them.

Then Lanik and Vrba added that the killings were not yet over by any means. "We saw the guards expand the facilities. Obviously, they're preparing to murder even more Jews in Auschwitz very soon. Our guess is that the Hungarian Jews are next. We overheard one of the Nazis saying 'We're ready for the Hungarian sausage now.' "

Rabbi Weissmandl realized exactly what this meant. The deportation of Hungarian Jews to Auschwitz was imminent.

BOMB THE RAIL LINES TO AUSCHWITZ!

The Working Group quickly wrote down the experiences of the two escapees in a thirty-page report. Rabbi Weissmandl composed a separate twelve-page summary in

Hebrew and added a heart-rending appeal for help. Included was a call for specific action that he was to repeat many times over the next few months: "Bomb the rail lines leading to Auschwitz!"

It was, after all, a very logical demand. The Allies were now flying regular bombing missions over German-held territory, including Poland, where Auschwitz was located. If they would simply send one fighter mission over Auschwitz and bomb the rail lines leading to Auschwitz-Birkenau–or the gas chambers themselves–the death machine would be severely crippled. The deportations and mass killings would be halted for at least a while, or even stopped for good. Furthermore, the attack would benefit the Allied war effort as well, since the Germans sent many trainloads of soldiers and ammunition over the very same rail line.

Rabbi Weissmandl managed to smuggle out exact maps and charts, obtained through his contacts, showing the layout of Auschwitz and the rail lines leading to it. He also provided information about when the trains loaded with Jews arrived each day. Accompanying each message sent (at great expense) to the outside world was the same plea, stated over and over: "Bomb the railroad tracks!"

The Sternbuchs and Vaad Hatzalah rushed the information to contacts in New York like Rabbi Avraham Kalmanowitz and Moreinu Yaakov Rosenheim. They, in turn, put intense pressure on their political allies in Washington and elsewhere. Finally, in June, the request reached the American State Department.

A month went by with no answer. During that time, one hundred and twenty-five thousand Jews were put to death at Auschwitz-Birkenau.

EXCUSES AND THE KILLING GOES ON

During the summer of 1944, John Pehle, the head of the War Refugee Board that had been belatedly created by President Roosevelt, formally asked the United States War Department to start bombing the Auschwitz rail lines as soon as possible. John J. McCloy, Assistant Secretary of War, retorted that the bombing would not be helpful, because the Germans would quickly repair the damage. He ignored the fact that Allied bombing was halting German rail transports elsewhere throughout Europe.

A week later, Pehle tried again. This time McCloy responded that Auschwitz was too far away for Allied planes to reach and that trying to bomb it would be hazardous.

Actually, Allied planes controlled the skies by that time and faced few challenges. And just eight days after McCloy's assertions, four hundred and fifty-two B-17 bombers took off from Allied bases in Italy to bomb Nazi positions. They came within ten miles of Auschwitz. In another three minutes' flying time they would have reached it. But they received no orders to go further.

A month later, over a hundred Allied bombers came within five miles of Auschwitz. It was a clear day, and the planes scored direct hits on their designated targets. Only one plane was lost in the raid. Yet Auschwitz remained unharmed, and the railroad lines stayed intact.

In September, 1944, a bomb did hit Auschwitz–entirely by accident. A force of B-17 bombers had been attacking a nearby munitions factory. One plane flew slightly off course, and when it dropped its payload, the bomb landed on Auschwitz, as a photograph of the event clearly demonstrated.

Aside from this one unintentional instance, Auschwitz was not hit by Allied planes, nor was rail traffic to it disrupted. Pleas to commence the bombing kept flowing to the War

Department. Each time the reply was that this mission would be both unsafe and militarily impossible.

The evidence proves otherwise.

There were those who feared that bombing Auschwitz would cause the deaths of many Jewish inmates there. But Auschwitz survivors later said this shouldn't have been a major issue. "We kept praying the Allies would bomb Auschwitz," one inmate recalled. "We knew some of us might be killed. But we were all slated to be killed by the Nazis anyway, and if the gas chambers had been knocked out of commission, further murders would have been avoided." So the Auschwitz prisoners kept scanning the skies for planes that never appeared.

Meanwhile, the gassing and killings were being accelerated. The Nazi overseers seemed in a frenzied rush, as if they had to complete a cherished task before time ran out. To them, it didn't apparently matter much whether or not they lost the war, just as long as all the Jews were murdered before it was all over.

A SELFLESS PROPOSAL

Seeing that his bombing proposal was meeting with no positive response, Rabbi Weissmandl sought other approaches. He concentrated on somehow finding a way to destroy the rail lines through other means, perhaps by dynamiting them. But who would be able to position the dynamite correctly under the tracks?

The members of the Working Group were heatedly discussing this issue when a young man entered the room. Rabbi Weissmandl recognized him as Yankel Lowy, a student at the Nitra Yeshivah. Lowy listened to the deliberations for a while and then raised his hand to attract attention.

"Can I suggest something?" he said. "There seems to be

one sure way to blow up the tracks." The others listened attentively.

"The train always enters a long tunnel on its way to the concentration camp, doesn't it? If the train is sabotaged while passing through the tunnel, it will have a devastating effect. If someone sneaks into the engine of the train with some dynamite, and explodes it at the right time, we'll achieve our goal."

"But how can someone get dynamite onto the train?" someone asked.

"By hiding it in his clothing," Lowy said.

"Yes, but then that person will be blown to bits, along with the engine."

"True. But I know someone who is willing to do it anyway."

"And who is that?"

"Me," said Lowy. "Just tell me when."

The members of the group stared at him in shock and admiration.

Finally, Rabbi Weissmandl spoke. "That is incredibly brave of you, my son. I wish there were more like you among us. We greatly appreciate your suggestion, especially your willingness to die for our people. Maybe it won't be necessary. We were just considering another approach, which would get the same results, without costing your life. Still, we thank you for your ideas and your courage. You've given all of us the lift to keep going in our work."

As it turned out, the Working Group used neither scheme. It was decided that if the Jews were caught trying to blow up the train, the Nazis would take their usual bloodthirsty reprisals. At the time, twenty-five thousand Slovakian Jews were still living in relative safety, and the Working Group couldn't risk their being killed by vengeful Nazis.

A HALT AT LAST

It was the inmates of Auschwitz themselves, the ones least physically equipped to take action, who finally took the step no one else had dared take. On October 7, 1944, dynamite smuggled in by female camp prisoners, a particle at a time, was detonated, blowing up one of the crematoria. The Nazis were stunned, and the killings stopped soon afterwards.

By this time, too, the daily shipments of Jews from Budapest to Auschwitz had also ceased. Neither dynamite nor bombs had accomplished this. Rather, it was due to the efforts of one remarkable person who had taken up Rabbi Weissmandl's challenge to act. A copy of the Auschwitz Protocols and the follow-up report on Hungarian deportations had finally found its way, weeks later, to George Mantello, an amateur Jewish diplomat and outstanding rescue leader. Mantello had then used all his varied contacts to gain vast publicity in the Swiss press for the report's horrific details. The resulting furor had stirred the nations in the free world to at last condemn Germany in unison for its barbaric crimes against the Jews. This gave Admiral Horthy the political muscle to order an end to the deportation of Jews from Hungary.

As the Russian army approached Auschwitz, the Nazis began forcibly marching some one hundred thousand feeble, starving Jews from the camp to locations in Germany. Many died of exhaustion and disease along the way.

On January 27, 1945, the Russians finally liberated what was left of the Auschwitz-Birkenau camp. The reign of unspeakable terror there–one that had taken the lives of over a million men, women and children, and had subjected thousands of others to the vilest forms of torture–was at long last over.

By this time, many of Rabbi Weissmandl's closest relatives and dearest companions had become victims of Auschwitz as well. And Rabbi Weissmandl had come perilously close to joining them himself.

TERROR RETURNS TO SLOVAKIA

In the fall of 1944, the long period of grace for Slovakian Jewry came to an end. With the Russian army drawing near, many Slovakian citizens, both Jews and non-Jews, dared to revolt against the pro-Nazi government. After fierce fighting, the revolt was crushed. As always, the Nazis sought to avenge this insult. As always, the Jews bore the brunt of the sadistic reprisals.

The two years of respite ended abruptly, as the deportations suddenly resumed. The remaining Slovakian Jews were rounded up and sent to Auschwitz in groups. Dieter Wisliceny was no longer available to slow the process. The Nazis had replaced him with a ruthless tyrant named Alois Brunner (now living in safety under the protection of the Syrian government), whose hatred for the Jews was so overwhelming that no bribe could deter his murderous mission.

The deportations began in the smaller cities, such as Nitra. The *yeshivah* there, which had still been functioning under Rabbi Ungar's direction, was shut down. On September 7, 1944, Rabbi Weissmandl, his wife and his five children (four daughters and one son) were arrested. So were Rabbi Ungar and his students. They and the other Jews of Nitra, as well as Jews from other territories in Slovakia, were taken to a detention camp in the city of Sered. From there they would be sent to Auschwitz.

When the members of the Working Group in Pressburg heard that Rabbi Weissmandl had been seized, they were grief-stricken. How could they possibly function in this crisis without him? Using their political contacts, they managed to secure permission for Rabbi Weissmandl to come to Pressburg, claiming they needed him to help compile important lists of Slovakian Jews for the government. However, the permission was granted for one night only.

Rabbi Weissmandl knew better than to return to the folds of the Nazi death grip. Instead, he went into hiding and made use of his time to seek help for Slovakia's beleaguered Jews.

Among those whose assistance he solicited were the heads of the Catholic Church, who were revered figures in Slovakia. Jozef Tiso, the country's leader, was a parish priest, and the threat of excommunication from the Church might have prompted him to abandon the deportations.

Rabbi Weissmandl approached the Church leaders under no illusions about their willingness to help. He had already sought their aid several times before, with discouraging results. In 1942, when he had first learned of the mass killings of the Jews in Poland, he had spent hours composing a letter to Pope Pius XII. Writing in the name of the rabbis of Poland and Slovakia, he had strongly urged the Vatican to condemn the cruel treatment of the Jews in clear terms. A messenger had been bribed to bring the letter to the Pope's aides and to return with their reply.

The Vatican had indeed protested the expulsions and killings to the Slovakian government. But its letter strongly implied that the Church was mainly interested in saving the lives of those Jews who had converted to Catholicism. Jews who remained Jews, it indicated, were not to be a matter of concern.

President Tiso had taken the Vatican's letter very seriously. He had subsequently ordered that those Jews who had converted would indeed be separated from other Jews and treated humanely. This answer had satisfied the Vatican. There had been no subsequent protests from the Pope when thousands of Slovakian Jews were expelled in April and May of 1942.

In 1943, when rumors arose that the deportations were about to resume, Rabbi Weissmandl had persuaded his father-in-law Rabbi Ungar to meet with Bishop Kmetko of Nitra and ask for his help.

The Bishop had agreed to the meeting, but his response had been chilling: "Yes, they are going to send all of you away, every Jew, from the youngest to the oldest. They are going to kill every one of you. And you deserve to die! After all, you killed the founder of our religion. Now you come and ask me to save you. Well, there is only one way you can be saved, my good rabbi, and that is by announcing your acceptance of our religion and its leader. When you Jews are ready to convert, then I will do everything I can to make the government stop these expulsions."

There were, indeed, some Catholic leaders, such as Angelo Roncalli (the Bishop of Turkey, who in 1958 became Pope John XXIII), who did their best to save Jews. Individual Catholics also risked their lives to hide Jews from the authorities. But the Pope himself said nothing. He remained strangely silent during the Jews' darkest hours. Though some claim that he privately urged the Nazis to spare the Jews, he made no public plea until mid-1944. In 1944, when the Hungarian Jews were being rounded up and sent to death camps, Jewish groups beseeched him to broadcast a denunciation of the killings. Instead of doing so, he sent a telegram to the Hungarian government, vaguely disapproving of persecution based on "race." He did not use the term "Jew" at all.

Now, to save the remaining Jews of Slovakia, Rabbi Weissmandl was once again turning in desperation to the Church. He managed to gain an audience with Monsignor Guiseppe Burzio, the Papal Nuncio (representative) in Budapest, Hungary.

"Your Eminence," he began. "I have just come from the camp at Sered where thousands of Slovakian Jews have been rounded up. Each day, another trainload of Jews is sent to the death camps at Auschwitz. I beg of you, sir, do something!"

Monsignor Burzio said nothing.

After several awkward moments, Rabbi Wissmandl went on. "Sir, all religions hold life dear. You have to help stop this mad slaughter. Perhaps you've heard that Cardinal Seredi of Hungary threatened Admiral Horthy with excommunication if he continued expelling Hungarian Jews. If you send the same message to President Tiso, it might have a dramatic effect. We would be eternally grateful to you."

Burzio drummed his fingers on the table, avoiding Rabbi Weissmandl's penetrating stare. Then he shook his head. "First of all," he said, "let me remind you that today is Sunday. And on Sunday, we do not deal with unholy matters."

Rabbi Weissmandl was stunned beyond belief. Could the Nuncio really have called the rescue of Jews from the death camps an "unholy matter"? With what kind of man was he dealing?

Nevertheless, he pressed his point. "Your Eminence, we Jews are all going to be slaughtered. Is the blood of thousands of innocent children a minor detail to you? Again, I plead with you. Take action! If you do, the Almighty will surely bless you."

With that, and the image of his detained wife and children in his mind, Rabbi Weissmandl broke down in tears.

The Papal Nuncio was not moved. Coldly, he rose and spoke with the slicing sharpness of a cutlass. "There is no such thing as blood of innocent Jewish children. All Jewish blood is guilty, because you killed our savior! And don't talk of Cardinal Seredi to me. Seredi himself should be excommunicated! Who asked him to meddle on behalf of you Jews? As for you, Rabbi Weissmandl, you are just another lowly Jew. You have some nerve coming here to see me. I will do what I should have done the moment you arrived. I'm calling the Gestapo to come arrest you."

"Sir," said Rabbi Weissmandl, "you are a disgrace to your

religion, and to all religions. May the Almighty smite you many times over for your cursed arrogance."

The Nuncio's face tightened, and he seemed ready to strangle Rabbi Weissmandl on the spot. But Rabbi Weissmandl wasn't about to let anything like that happen. He climbed out a window and ran off before the Nuncio could carry out his threat.

Rabbi Weissmandl then hid out with other members of the Working Group for a while. However, the Nazi in charge of the Slovakian deportations, Alois Brunner, was determined to have the distinguished rabbi in his custody. He ordered his men to find Rabbi Weissmandl before the latter had a chance to warn the Jews of Pressburg that they, too, would soon be deported.

The soldiers managed to locate Rabbi Weissmandl and, after arresting him, brought him to Nazi headquarters. There, before him, smiling cynically, was Brunner.

"So, Rabbi, we finally have you back among us."

Rabbi Weissmandl reasoned that he might as well speak his mind. They would probably kill him now no matter what, so he had nothing to lose.

"Yes, it looks like I'm now in your power," he told Brunner. "But just how long do you think your power is going to last?"

"What do you mean by that?"

"Let's be frank, Herr Commandant. Germany is losing the war. The Russians are closing in on you from one side, the British and Americans from the other. It's only a matter of time before you are caught. So after the war, you'll be tried and hanged."

Brunner shrugged. "Then I might as well enjoy myself now and continue killing Jews."

"On the contrary," Rabbi Weissmandl said. "If you stop this mad policy now and halt these deportations, the Allies might be more lenient with you someday. We Jews will be the first to testify to your change of heart. In other words, if you help us now, we might come to your aid when the war is over."

"No, you won't," said Brunner. "Because by then, all you Jews will be dead."

This cold-blooded sadist hadn't an ounce of sympathy in his heart. Still, Rabbi Weissmandl kept trying to sway him. For over two hours, he put forth arguments, sometimes even banging on Brunner's desk in excitement. He poured all his passionate persuasiveness into a last effort to save his fellow Slovakian Jews.

Finally, Brunner flashed his cynical smile and sneered. "I must say one thing for you, rabbi. You certainly are persistent. I want to remember you for a long time. Come with me."

He took Rabbi Weissmandl to a special studio, where he had the Nazi photographer snap no fewer than twenty-two poses of him, from every possible angle. "Good," said Brunner.

"Now we have a complete record of exactly how you look. That way, we'll certainly be able to identify and recapture you if you ever manage to slip away from us on your next trip."

"Trip?" said Rabbi Weissmandl. "Where to?"

"Auschwitz," said Brunner.

Shortly afterwards, Rabbi Weissmandl and his entire family, now reunited, were loaded onto a cattle car to Auschwitz, along with hundreds of others from Sered. They seemed about to make the same ill-fated journey that so many of their doomed countrymen had made before them.

THE DECISION OF A LIFETIME

Rabbi Weissmandl entered the cattle car with almost nothing in his possession, but he was not totally emptyhanded. He knew exactly what was in store for him once the train reached its destination. He had therefore come prepared.

For weeks before his attempted escape to Pressburg, he had been readying his students at Nitra for just such an emergency as this. He'd given them tips on how to escape from a speeding train and had supplied them with parts of a hacksaw blade for possible future use.

Rabbi Weissmandl had hidden one of these saw blades inside his shoe. When the right time came, he would employ it.

The train rumbled along, and the Jews crammed inside stood crushed together in the foul, sweltering heat. They received no food or water. The atmosphere inside was oppressive. Some of the older, weaker passengers had already sunk to the ground. Night was falling. If Rabbi Weissmandl was going to act, the time was now.

The Nazis had locked the train door shut. If he could somehow get over to the lock and saw it off, he might be able to create an exit passage. But in this mass of humanity, how could he push his way to the lock without starting a riot and attracting the Nazis' attention?

Left without any alternatives, and thinking quickly, Rabbi Weissmandl pretended to be sick to his stomach. His appearance caused the other Jews to avoid him as he rushed to the corner of the car. Once there, he settled down and began sawing away furiously. Somehow, from the stirrings of his restless soul, he summoned up a burst of manic energy. Slowly, stubbornly, he got the lock to loosen, and it began to give way.

"Baruch Hashem," he whispered.

The train door swung open just far enough for one person at a time to squeeze through to safety. Rabbi Weissmandl triumphantly looked around for the rest of his family. They had become separated from him in the crowd. His wife and his five children seemed so frightened, so fragile huddled together like that. Could they make it to safety?

"Quick!" he motioned to his wife, pointing to the train door and beckoning them closer.

His wife began moving forward. Just then the train swerved slightly, and she and the children were thrown back. The youngest ones began to whimper.

Once again, Rabbi Weissmandl urged them towards him. But now the other passengers, jostled by the ragged journey, began pressing in on them. The children huddled closer to their mother. They were too frightened to move.

Rabbi Weissmandl's wife looked at him and pointed to the children. "It's impossible," she said.

Rabbi Weissmandl stood frozen. Maybe his wife was right. The children looked petrified. Some of them might easily die in the getaway attempt. On the other hand, if they stayed on the train, they would probably be killed once they got to Auschwitz. But then again, the Russians might very well liberate the death camp soon. Perhaps they could survive until then. Still, it might be better to take a chance on making it out of the train, even if recapture was probable.

"Come," Rabbi Weissmandl implored his wife.

But again the children refused to budge. Shaking her head mournfully, she answered back, "I can't."

Rabbi Weissmandl lowered his head in agony. What should he do next? How could he stay on the train, when the Nazis were sure to torture and kill him, their hated enemy, at Auschwitz? Yet, how could he abandon his family to a gruesome fate? If he escaped from the train, he might be able to continue his rescue work elsewhere. But how could he go on if his family was wrenched away from him?

It was a terrible dilemma, an excruciating choice. But he had to decide soon. The seconds were ticking away, and as it grew light outside, the Nazis would be more likely to notice his escape and recapture him.

He bowed his head in prayer, asking Hashem to help him choose wisely.

In the end, he remained a man of action. With his heart pounding, he positioned himself above the exit passage in the train car. Then bracing himself, he slipped through. As he hit the ground, he instantly rolled over several times deliberately, thus absorbing the shock of the fall. Then he scurried into a nearby patch of bushes to safety.

Carefully, he peeked through the shrubbery towards the train tracks. He was hoping that others, including his family, had taken his lead and followed suit. Perhaps all they'd needed was an example, a Nachshon Ben Aminadav to show them the way. He held his breath and squinted into the darkness.

No. Nothing stirred.

They hadn't made it.

He watched as the train rolled on, becoming a vague dot on the brightening horizon, and then disappearing. It took with it all those he loved most dearly in the world. And he knew it was most probably carrying them to an unspeakable fate.

He never saw them again.

Later, Rabbi Weissmandl learned that other members of the Working Group, including Mrs. Gisi Fleischmann, had also been sent to Auschwitz. Their friends and associates had tried every possible means of saving them, but they'd failed, and Mrs. Fleischmann and the others perished in the death camps, too.

Rabbi Weissmandl's world was shattered, almost beyond repair. But his life somehow went on.

He had jumped off the train near a village not far from Pressburg. After a treacherous journey, and after being turned away from several possible hiding spots, he found temporary shelter with a villager. He knew he could not stay there long, so he proceeded to carry out an emergency plan that had been devised long before.

DANGER AND DEVOTION IN THE BUNKER

Rabbi Weissmandl had known of a secret hiding place for Slovakian Jews, a bunker set up by a non-Jew named Janku Provaznik in the yard of his Pressburg home. Jews had been concealed there as early as 1941, and in 1944, seventeen Jews were living in the bunker.

Because of his anti-Nazi work, Rabbi Weissmandl knew he was in constant danger of arrest. He had therefore arranged some months before to be taken to the bunker if his life was ever in peril. According to the plan, Rabbi Weissmandl was to contact a non-Jewish printer named Natali, who would bring him to the bunker. Even though Natali's son was a Jew-hating Gestapo man, Natali himself risked his life time and time again to spirit Jews to safety.

While he was still at the villager's house, Rabbi Weissmandl asked a girl from the neighborhood to bring a coded letter to Natali who lived nearby. Natali knew that he, in turn, was to bring it to the bunker. He quickly did so, and those hiding inside immediately recognized it as having come from their colleague Rabbi Weissmandl. Natali then returned to the girl, who was just about to leave. Together, they took the last train back to the village, and Natali and Rabbi Weissmandl set out on foot for the bunker. After an exhausting trip, they reached it without incident. Those in the bunker welcomed Rabbi Weissmandl warmly and were gratified to see he was still alive. They'd heard that Alois Brunner had posted a large reward for his capture.

Yes, Rabbi Weissmandl was indeed alive, but he was deeply depressed. Day after day, he wept over his separation from his family. He also agonized over the fate of his fellow Jews. "So many are dead," he kept repeating. "If only I'd tried harder to ransom them. Why didn't I do more?"

Among the others in the bunker was Rabbi Menachem Mendel Halberstam, the beloved Chassidic Rebbe of Stropkov.

The Rebbe was a holy, impressive figure, and his presence had a soothing effect on the others there. Rabbi Weissmandl also looked up to him, and came to him with his feelings of guilt.

The Rebbe listened carefully. Then he smiled and said comfortingly, "Michoel, no other person on earth, Jew or non-Jew, has done more to help his fellow man than you. Thousands, even millions, have died, it is true. But without you, so many others would have perished, too. Don't blame yourself. Don't give in to depression. Have faith. You have many more years ahead of you, and much good work yet to do."

The Rebbe's words were like a balm, slowly reinvigorating him. Rabbi Weissmandl still had melancholic moments, but he also looked forward to the future now, praying for the war to be over in the quickest possible time.

Yet, even while he was hidden in the bunker, he managed to carry on his acts of *chessed*. With the help of a Jew named Mr. Funk, who disguised himself as a non-Jew and regularly ventured into town, Rabbi Weissmandl was able to keep in touch with Jews in other bunkers and to direct essential funds to them.

Life in the bunker was numbingly difficult. The inhabitants remained indoors for weeks at a time, seated uncomfortably in confined quarters. That way they hoped to escape detection by the Nazis, who continually searched the area.

Once, an inhabitant who had been standing guard came rushing back to the bunker.

"Nazi soldiers!" he shouted. "I saw a whole group of them. They're making a house-to-house search of the area. And they're coming right this way!"

This was the moment they'd all been dreading, the moment of truth. Families drew closer. Others wept softly.

One of the men turned to the Rebbe of Stropkov. "Rebbe, is there anything we can do?"

The Rebbe, immersed in the studies that always occupied him in the bunker, simply waved off the problem. "There is nothing to be afraid of," he said. "As long as we have full trust in Hashem, they will not find us."

The others were relieved to hear this, and the atmosphere of panic began dissipating. Inwardly, they wondered how the Rebbe could be so sure of himself. After all, the Nazis were almost at their doorstep now. It would be only a matter of minutes before they barged into the bunker. But if this holy man said there was no need to worry . . .

The Nazis marched up to the house of Janku Provaznik and rang the bell. At this, Provaznik's guard dog inside the house began to bark and snarl ferociously. One of the soldiers took his gun and aimed it at the dog. Once the dog was taken care of, they would storm the house and undoubtedly come to the yard–where the bunker was located.

"Wait!"

The Nazis spun around. A man approached them, a neighbor of Provaznik.

"Don't shoot," he told the Nazis. "Why waste your bullets on a fine dog like that? Save them for the Jews. Besides, there's no reason to bother looking inside the house. Provaznik doesn't keep any Jews there. Everyone knows he's an anti-Semite. He'd rather kill a Jew than let one anywhere near here."

Hearing that, the soldiers smiled. They tipped their helmets to the man and left.

Inside the bunker, the Jews prayed and waited. And waited. Eventually, the sounds outside died away. They realized that no one was coming. The Rebbe had been right.

Normally, life in the bunker was less dramatic. The men used their time to study Torah, learning from the few *sefarim* they had managed to bring with them. Provaznik brought them all food and clothing, and the girls in the bunker helped with the cooking and laundry. Though the existence was a meager one, there were even some celebrations, on a minor scale.

Purim was one such occasion. The girls baked special dishes, and they even performed the *mitzvah* of *mishloach manos* in the best way they could. There was one single cube of sugar in the bunker, and everyone took turns passing it to the next person. In this way they fulfilled the *mitzvah*, if only symbolically. Soon, they hoped, they would be able to celebrate their own victory over a hated enemy.

A BITTERSWEET FREEDOM

One day, the inhabitants were surprised to receive a visit from Dr. Rudolf Kastner. He had come to the bunker to explain that a deal had been made. Jews hiding in bunkers would be freed as part of a prisoner exchange. Those in the Provaznik bunker would be sent to Switzerland via truck.

Soon after, the truck appeared, driven by a Gestapo officer. The Jews were reluctant to go, fearing a trick. Eventually, though, they decided to board. After a treacherous journey and many delays, the truck (which included about sixty Jews from various bunkers) arrived in Switzerland shortly after Pesach of 1945.

Then the strain of the war finally caught up with Rabbi Weissmandl. His many exertions, and the anguish he felt at the loss of every Jewish soul, had taken a heavy toll on his health. Shortly after coming to Switzerland, he suffered a major heart attack, which led to a lengthy hospitalization. It was at this time, too, that he learned that his wife and children had indeed been killed at Auschwitz and that his father-in-law Rabbi Ungar had died while hiding from the Nazis in the forests of Slovakia.

But there was also some good news. A number of the students of the Nitra Yeshivah, including his brother-in-law Rabbi Sholom Moshe Ungar and close Talmid Rabbi Jonah Forst, had managed to survive the war. They re-established contact with each other and joined together to reopen the yeshivah with about fifty students. The old *yeshivah* building had been destroyed during the war, so the *talmidim* used the house of Nitra's former *dayan* as their study hall. Rabbi Weissmandl was greatly encouraged by their determination to revive the *yeshivah* and its traditions. Although he was still confined to bed, he wrote from Switzerland that he would help them in any way he could.

NEW LIVES IN THE NEW WORLD

Soon it became clear that, even though the Nazis had been defeated, it was still not safe for Jews to live in Eastern Europe. Anti-Semitic incidents made Rabbi Weissmandl search for a new location for the Nitra Yeshivah. After much deliberation, he traveled to the United States and eventually found a site for the *yeshivah* in Somerville, New Jersey. The students left Slovakia and, after spending some time in France, arrived in the United States towards the end of 1946.

Meanwhile, Rabbi Weissmandl had begun rebuilding his own life. He still grieved for those who had died, but his meetings with the Satmar Rebbe, like those earlier with the Rebbe of Stropkov, significantly increased his peace of mind. He was remarried, to Rabbi Sholom Moshe Ungar's sister-in-law, and built a new family of five sons and one daughter. He also developed new educational ideas.

There were few *yeshivos gedolos* in America at this time, and Rabbi Weissmandl wanted to establish a new trend in *chinuch*. He envisioned a *yeshivah* community that was an entity in itself, one in which *bnei yeshivah* could learn, work and raise families all within a true Torah atmosphere.

As he saw it, if *bnei yeshivah* settled in the large metropolitan centers of America, they would easily become influenced by the non-Jewish culture of their surroundings. Therefore, he sought to build a self-contained Torah community, located in a small farming village. There, young Jewish men would learn without distractions until they married. Then those who showed special promise in their Torah studies would continue their all-day learning. Others would live and work in the village settlement, producing agricultural products or being employed in trades like printing. These workers would support the *yeshivah* and raise their families in accordance with Torah ideals. In such a settlement, a *ben Torah* could enjoy a self-sufficient life without facing interference from non-Torah influences.

UNSETTLING PROBLEMS

Ever the pragmatist, still itching to get things moving, Rabbi Weissmandl now drove himself to translate his visions into reality. He found an ideal spot for such a *yeshivah* settlement in Mount Kisco, New York, and the Nitra Yeshivah students relocated there. However, new problems arose. The cost of the move left the *yeshivah* with a considerable financial debt, and some of the programs had to be curtailed. In addition, the *yeshivah* evoked antagonism from the local neighbors, especially the secular Jews who did not want to be identified with these obviously religious young men with long beards and dangling *peyos*. At one point, it seemed likely the *yeshiva* would have to close.

At that juncture, a philanthropist offered him a great deal of money that would have solved the financial difficulties. However, there were strings attached, and these would have challenged Rabbi Weissmandl's educational principles. He therefore sent the man a letter of thanks for his generous offer but firmly turned it down. There was no point in winning financing for a *yeshivah* that did not live up to his standards.

Eventually, other funds were found, easing the financial

strain. And, with the help of non-Jews like Mrs. Baldwin (the wife of a *New York Times* correspondent), who lectured the local inhabitants on appreciating Rabbi Weissmandl's stature, community opposition to the *yeshivah* subsided. The Mount Kisco *yeshivah* survived, and it is still very much in existence today, under the capable supervision of Rabbi Solomon Ungar.

THE FINAL YEARS

Though Rabbi Weissmandl's life was now centered around the new *yeshivah* and the *shiurim* he gave there, he could not forget the overwhelming tragedy of the Holocaust years. Time and again, he spoke to his students about the bitter lessons of the war. He told them of how many Jews, including a good number of Orthodox Jews, had turned their backs on those crying for help.

The questions in his mind—primarily, "Where were our fellow Jews when we needed them?—continued to haunt him. He began searching for the letters he had written during the war, letters which gave proof of his own desperate search for assistance. And he kept demanding of Jewish groups, "Why didn't you answer when we called you?"

Rabbi Weissmandl was especially critical of the Socialist Zionist movement. He felt it had concentrated throughout the war on planning for a postwar Jewish state rather than on the immediate task of saving Jewish lives. As a result, he indignantly opposed the creation of the secular state of Israel.

Eventually, he began compiling his letters and documents into a book, which he called *Min Hametzar* (*From the Depths*). It described his rescue attempts during the war, and the frustrations he had experienced. It was an emotional, deep-felt *sefer*, and though it was later published, it was to remain unfinished.

By the mid-1950s, Rabbi Weissmandl looked much older

than his years. The turmoil and torment of the war years, the pangs of guilt that still occasionally plagued him and the burden of sustaining the *yeshivah* in Mount Kisco had all taken their toll. He suffered several heart attacks and was once again hospitalized.

A student came to visit him, and they discussed *Divrei Torah* for a while. Then he asked the student to excuse him, for he felt the need to rest. The student quickly took his leave. As he was doing so, he noticed Rabbi Weissmandl reaching for an old, worn *sefer* that lay on a nearby desk.

Then the student recognized it. It was a volume of Rabbeinu Bachya's commentaries on the Torah, the very same *sefer* he had bought with the money his grandfather had given him. It was as if he was, at the twilight of his life, reclaiming a link to the peaceful, scholarly world of his youth.

By the time the student returned to the *yeshivah*, the word had come: Rabbi Michoel Ber Weissmandl had passed away. It was the 6th of Kislev, in the year 5718 (1957), and Rabbi Weissmandl was only fifty-four years old.

Like Shlomo Hamelech, Rabbi Weissmandl lived for little more than half a century. Yet that short lifetime contained barely a wasted moment. It had been dedicated in full to Hashem and His people.

The inscription on his tombstone speaks movingly of his undying devotion to Torah and his unflagging commitment to saving his fellow Jews. He may personally have believed that his efforts were inadequate. Nevertheless, the thousands he saved, and the multitudes he inspired, emphatically disagreed. They saw him as a man of unimaginable courage, a rabbi who dared take on a foe of unrivaled menace almost single-handedly.

In the final analysis, by setting the highest standards of selflessness for himself, and embodying the purest values of the Torah, Rabbi Michoel Ber Weissmandl succeeded in living a meritorious life beyond any shadow of a doubt.

A CRY FROM THE HEART

RABBI AVRAHAM KALMANOWITZ

Rabbi Avrohom Kalmanowitz was a Mirrer *rosh yeshivah* who helped the entire *yeshivah* escape to Shanghai, where he supported them throughout the war. He was also most effective in influencing the American government to assist in the rescue of all the Jews of occupied Europe.

2   A CRY FROM THE HEART

RABBI AVRAHAM KALMANOWITZ

THE CAR CAME TO A SCREECHING HALT, AND FROM IT EMERGED
two distinguished *rabbonim* in traditional black garb. A few
local residents recognized them as Rabbi Avraham Kalmanowitz, the director of the Mirrer Yeshivah, and his younger
colleague Rabbi Gedaliah Schorr, who would later become
rosh yeshivah of Yeshivah Torah Vodaath.

With a sturdy gait, they hastened into the stately *shul*
building before them, passing open-mouthed onlookers on
their way. Their arrival had raised eyebrows for a very obvious
reason. They had come on the holy *Shabbos*, a day on which
these devout Torah scholars would normally never dream of
driving. With the war on, though, the unexpected had become the norm.

Rabbi Kalmanowitz had just received a message from
Rabbi Michoel Ber Weissmandl, his associate in rescue work
a continent away. There was a pressing and immediate need
for funds. A chance still existed that the lives of European Jews
could be ransomed. According to Rabbi Weissmandl, the

Nazis were talking of sparing Jews if a sizable bribe were paid. But the offer would not remain on the table indefinitely. The Nazis could change their minds at any time. So the Jews of America had to make use of their relative affluence and help supply the funds–right away!

The clarion call had brought Rabbi Kalmanowitz and Rabbi Schorr to this wealthy New York congregation in quest of donations. It was only one of several *shuls* they would be approaching that *Shabbos*, located all over the city. And since the funds were so urgently required to save lives, obtaining them became the supreme consideration. Because of the need to reach as many congregations as possible, driving on *Shabbos* became not only permissible but mandatory.

Coming upon a congregant in the lobby, Rabbi Kalmanowitz said in his fragmented English, "Please, we would like to see the *gabbai*."

The *gabbai* was located and asked what the worthy rabbis wanted.

"We wish to speak to the people in the *shul*," Rabbi Kalmanowitz explained. "It is very, very important."

The *gabbai* replied that this was something for the *shul* president to deal with and summoned him. The president, in turn, said that the *shul's* rabbi had to make the final decision.

Meanwhile, time was wasting.

The rabbi eventually came to the lobby and greeted his guests. When he heard Rabbi Kalmanowitz's request, though, he looked doubtful.

"I'm afraid we don't allow visitors off the street to address the congregation," he said. "Maybe you could come back during the week, and we'll try to fit you into our schedule."

"But Jews are in danger of dying," said Rabbi Schorr. "If we wait, even a few days—"

"I understand. But I'm sorry. We can't start making exceptions." The rabbi began walking away.

"Wait!" Rabbi Kalmanowitz raced over to him. "Please, I beg of you. Allow me to say only *one* thing to the people. Just one word!"

The rabbi's curiosity was piqued. Only one word? How could one single word possibly accomplish anything?

"In the name of the Jews of Europe–please!"

The rabbi was by now wavering. "Well . . . all right. But only if you keep your promise. One word, no more. Our members don't like to be disturbed during the services."

The rabbi led them into the sanctuary and, once the Torah reading was finished, accompanied them to the *bimah*. He briefly introduced Rabbi Kalmanowitz and then remained at his side to make sure the visitor lived up to his agreement.

Trembling with emotion, Rabbi Kalmanowitz stepped forward. He shot a riveting stare around the room, as the congregants waited expectantly. Then suddenly, from the very core of his being, there emerged a single, shattering sound:

"Help!"

Then he collapsed.

The congregants gasped. A beat later, three doctors who were present rushed to the stricken rabbi's side. The rabbi of the *shul* remained skeptical, though, until the doctors reassured him that Rabbi Kalmanowitz had indeed fainted. With emergency treatment, the doctors managed to revive him. Soon he was back on his feet, as the congregants watched him in rapt attention.

"Are you all right?" asked the rabbi, now genuinely concerned.

"Me?" asked Rabbi Kalmanowitz. "You are concerned with me? Thank you, I am fine. But *gevalt*! So many of our fellow Jews in Europe are suffering. So many of them are dying. So many!"

He broke down in sobs.

Everyone waited as he regained his composure. When

he continued speaking, his voice took on an even more emotional tone than before.

"Yes, *rabbosai*! Here in America, a man faints, and people rush to help him. But there, in Europe, our brothers and sisters are falling by the hundreds and the thousands, and no one raises a finger to help! What is happening? How can we let this go on?"

The rabbi of the *shul* wasn't sure if he should allow this visitor to go on. After all, he had by now far exceeded his one-word limit. But as the Rabbi scanned his hushed membership, he saw clearly that Rabbi Kalmanowitz's emotional outburst had hit home. The people sensed that here was a truly holy individual who would do anything—travel on the *Shabbos*, jeopardize his own health—to save the lives of his fellow Jews. They were eager to hear a sage who obviously spoke from the heart.

The rabbi therefore said nothing and allowed Rabbi Kalmanowitz to proceed with his appeal. When it was over, the members responded by pledging amounts far beyond anyone's expectations.

Rabbi Kalmanowitz warmly thanked the throng for their generosity. However, he did not allow himself any time to gloat over his success. Moments later, he and Rabbi Schorr were on their way to yet another appeal in the next *shul*.

Those who worked alongside Rabbi Kalmanowitz during the war years remember him as a man in perpetual motion, a sage obsessed with saving Jews. Self-sacrifice was a key aspect of his character. To him, *hatzalah* was a non-negotiable priority, not a sideline. "He ate, slept and breathed only rescue, rescue, rescue," his close associate Rabbi Alex Weisfogel later recalled. And he threw himself into his efforts with an emotional intensity which had a great impact on others.

He was also incredibly persistent and would not take "No" for an answer, even from high-ranking American officials, when the welfare of trapped Jews was at stake.

"You might ask him to leave by the door and he would come back through the window," remembered John Pehle, head of the War Refugee Board, in characterizing Rabbi Kalmanowitz's tenacity.

He was a distinguished *talmid chacham*, a European *rav*, and the president of the prestigious Mirrer Yeshivah. Yet, Rabbi Kalmanowitz wouldn't think twice of working with any individual—be he a free-thinker, an irreligious Zionist or a non-Jew—who might help in his rescue crusade. And he would try any approach or tactic that might be effective, even if it cost him dearly in terms of money or physical well-being.

These efforts bore fruit. It can be claimed with good reason that, through the sum total of all his activities, Rabbi Avraham Kalmanowitz helped to save more European Jews than almost any other Jewish leader in America during the war years.

EARLY ACHIEVEMENTS

This dynamic *gadol* was born in Delatich, Poland, in 1891. His father Reb Aryeh Leib Kalmanowitz was a noted *baal mussar*, who made sure that his son received a superior Torah education. After learning at the Slobodka Yeshivah, Avraham became Rav in Rakov and head of a *kolel* he founded, as well as a leader of Agudath Israel of Poland. Later, he was chosen for the prestigious position of Rav of Tiktin, a city where such Torah giants as the Maharsha and Pnei Yehoshua had earlier served as spiritual leaders. Rabbi Kalmanowitz accepted this position under two conditions: that he be able to travel and raise funds on behalf of the Mirrer Yeshivah, of which he was president, and that the city support the *yeshivah* he planned to found there.

His leadership abilities were evident early on to all. When

a fire broke out in Tiktin, threatening to devour many wooden houses, the Jews of the town were near panic. They could not rely on the assistance of the local non-Jewish fire department, many of whose members had shown up at the scene dangerously drunk. There seemed no way of organizing a team to fight the growing inferno.

Suddenly, a commanding figure appeared on the roof of a building in the blaze's path. Rabbi Kalmanowitz had climbed up there to take charge personally of the fire-fighting effort.

From his vantage point, he had an excellent view of the situation, as well as a good sense of which way the winds were blowing. With crisp, emphatic commands, he indicated to the crowd below what should be done next. The sight of this sage giving direct, cool-headed instructions during the crisis sobered up the firemen, and Jews and non-Jews alike immediately accepted his authority. Working together under Rabbi Kalmanowitz's stewardship, they soon had the fire under control.

THE MIRACULOUS RESCUE OF MIR

With his natural flair for leadership, coupled with his outstanding scholarship, he was an obvious choice to become, at the youthful age of thirty-seven, the director of the world-famous Mirrer Yeshivah.

This illustrious Torah center had been founded in 1815. More recently, it had been blessed with such leaders as Rabbi Eliezer Yehuda Finkel, Rabbi Yerucham Levovitz and Rabbi Chaim Shmuelewitz, among others. The *yeshivah* had weathered two major fires during the 1800s, as well as temporary exile during World War I. Yet it had survived and grown, and by the 1930s it had gained international recognition as one of the foremost *yeshivos* in the world, spiritual home to hundreds of brilliant *talmidim*. Then World War II intervened.

The German invasion of Poland on September 1, 1939, meant that the glory days of the Polish *yeshivos*, including Mir, were over. When Communist Russia, by agreement with Germany, took control of eastern Poland, the future looked bleak indeed. The country was now split between the Jews' two foremost enemies. Surely, the *yeshivah* students, the cream of Polish Jewry, would be among their first targets. However, there now ensued a miraculous development, the first of many that would spare the lives of hundreds of *talmidim*.

For obscure political reasons, the pact dividing Poland between Germany and Russia had also stipulated that control of the Polish city of Vilna (where the Vilna Gaon resided in the 1700s) would be turned over to Lithuania. This seemed a peculiar move, since Lithuania hadn't even requested it. Time would soon prove it a prime example of *hashgachah pratis* (divine intervention).

The Russian forces marched into eastern Poland on *Tzom Gedaliah*, 1939. Mir was now under Soviet domination, and the residents encountered severe food shortages caused by the wild looting sprees of Russian soldiers. Even more alarming than the hunger were reports that *yeshivah* students would be exiled to Siberia. The charge against them? Subversion. On what basis? They had learned Torah, and their fealty to *Yiddishkeit* challenged the atheistic credo of Communism.

Quick decisions were needed, and the *rosh yeshivah*, in consultation with the older *talmidim*, made them. There was an immediate, desperate need to flee. But how? And where? The Russians were in control, and it was well known that no one was able to leave Soviet territory legally.

The answer, however, lay before them. Vilna! This beacon of Jewish learning, home to Rabbi Chaim Ozer Grodzensky and other *gedolim*, would prove a haven. It was in Lithuanian, not Russian, territory, and it had the benefit of an open border. Jews could enter without presenting any papers or encountering any restrictions.

Still, they could not risk any Russian interference. On the second of *Cheshvan*, 5700 (1939), in the very depths of the night, a massive evacuation began. Most Mirrer *talmidim* set out on a long but life-saving journey to Vilna. The remainder of the students, as well as their *rebbeim*, followed soon after. The Jewish citizens of Mir were heartbroken at their departure, but they realized it was necessary. Two years later, when Germany attacked on Russia, the Nazis conquered Mir. Within a year, almost all its remaining 9,000 Jews were killed.

Thousands of other students from various Polish *yeshivos* had also decided to use Vilna as a place of refuge and streamed into the city. This influx severely taxed the resources of Vilna's Jewish community. Nevertheless, Rabbi Chaim Ozer Grodzensky, the sick and aging *av bais din* of Vilna and world-renowned *gaon* and leader of *Klal Yisrael*, and his associates managed to provide for the students' physical and spiritual needs. Finding housing and food for all these young scholars during those chaotic times was anything but easy. Yet somehow, basic accommodations were obtained, and most importantly, the Torah learning continued unabated. The lectures and *shiurim* went on with even greater fervor than before. The *roshei yeshivah* and their *talmidim* realized that their Torah study was the essential factor sustaining them.

It was the students' hope that from Vilna they could secure passage to another country. However, for this they needed not only passports—which most *talmidim* were without—but also visas to pass through and then enter other lands. The United States was unwilling to broaden its quota system to allow admission of additional refugees, and England (in deference to the Arabs and their oil) was preventing Jews from settling in Eretz Yisrael. Thus, only a fortunate few were able to secure permission to leave.

One of these was Rabbi Kalmanowitz. As the Mirrer Yeshivah's main fund-raiser, he had visited the United States several times during the 1930s. With typical foresight, he had applied for American citizenship during these stays, thinking that it might one day prove useful. That day had now arrived, and his status allowed him to gain admittance to the United States when others were being turned away.

In April, 1940, after a difficult trip via Lithuania and Sweden (where he received the care and assistance of rescue leader Hans Lehmann), he arrived in New York. Eager to help his stranded students in any way possible, he commenced his tireless rescue work the very next day.

"Hashem has allowed me to arrive in the free world for a reason," he said. "I cannot afford to waste a minute."

Meanwhile, word came that Russia had apparently reconsidered, and was requesting that Lithuania turn over Vilna to her. In addition, Lithuania itself was falling under the domination of the Communists. Thus, even though the Mirrer Yeshivah *talmidim* had by this time moved from Vilna to the nearby city of Keidan in Lithuania, they were still affected by world events. On July 21, 1940, Lithuania buckled under Russian pressure and "requested" admission to the Soviet nation as one of its Republics. Those in Vilna were again to be under Russian control. Now the fate of the *yeshivah bachurim* who had earlier escaped exile to Siberia seemed to be looming again.

Some of the Mirrer Yeshivah administrators, including Rabbi Chaim Shmuelewitz, were at one point given the opportunity to obtain visas and thereby flee to safety. However, they refused all such offers. Either all their *talmidim* would leave with them, or they would all remain. The *yeshiva* could achieve a meaningful survival only if it remained a united entity. At this point, such a survival seemed highly improbable.

UNLIKELY VISAS

Rabbi Kalmanowitz, now based in New York, worked furiously to aid his precious *yeshivah* students, seeking all kinds of ways to find a safe haven for them. This required exit visas from Lithuania and end visas from a country willing to accept them. They also needed transit visas to pass through Japan, since Europe was already embroiled in war and the only escape route seemed to be via Siberia and Japan to the West, preferably the United States. The first priority, however, was to get them out of Russian-occupied Lithuania.

It was a pair of students from the Telshe Yeshiva in Poland, Nathan Gutwirth and Chaim Nussbaum, who found a break in the clouds. These Telshe students were originally from Holland. To see if their native land could assist them in leaving Lithuania, they made contact with Dr. I.P.J. de Dekker, the Dutch Ambassador to the Baltic States of Lithuania, Latvia and Estonia. Getting a visa to Holland itself might prove difficult. However, Gutwirth remembered that Holland had allowed free entry to Curacao, an island in the West Indies governed by the Dutch, who were seeking settlers there.

"Could you provide us with an end visa to Curacao?" he asked Dr. Dekker.

"You don't need a visa for Curacao," the Ambassador replied. "You could get a landing permit, but that could come only from the Governor of Curacao, and that would take time."

Gutwirth thought for a moment. "Could you please repeat that?"

"All I said was, Curacao doesn't require a visa, but—"

"Stop!" Gutwirth shouted. "That's all we need. Could you possibly put what you just said in writing?"

The Ambassador was fully aware of the charade being played in order to save lives, and he was willing to play along. The two Telshe students now had what they wanted–an

RABBI AVRAHAM KALMANOWITZ

official end visa, even if it wasn't quite the standard document. With such an "end visa," they now could save not only themselves but also their fellow *talmidim* in the *yeshivos.*

When members of the other *yeshivos* stranded in Lithuania heard of Gutwirth's coup, they asked him if he could secure Curacao visas for them as well. He assured them he would try.

"How many more visas do you want?" the Ambassador asked. "Two or three?"

"Well, yes . . . actually, two or three *hundred.*"

The Ambassador considered. He knew what was happening; he knew these Jews would never come to Curacao. It would have been very easy to refuse the request. Fortunately, though, he was sympathetic to the refugees' plight.

"All right, no problem," he said. "But I can't provide the visas for you here in Riga. I'll contact the Dutch consul in Kovno. His name is Zwartendijk. Go see him."

That Jon Zwartendijk was the Dutch representative in Kovno was itself a miraculous development. Zwartendijk was not a professional diplomat. Rather, he was a businessman, working for a reputable Dutch firm. Fortunately for the Jews, he had been asked to fill the post temporarily after the real consul had been dismissed as a Nazi sympathizer. The earlier consul had been an admirer of the Nazis and an ardent Jew-hater. Almost certainly, he would have rejected jeeringly the *yeshivah* students' request. Zwartendijk was, on the other hand, a humanitarian, and he proved most accommodating. He issued as many Curacao visas as were requested, covering over 2,000 Jews.

THE JAPANESE CONNECTION

However, their departure was not yet a sure thing, by any means. To gain access to the free world, the Jews would have to leave Vilna and travel through Russia to their desired destination. There was considerable doubt that Communist Russia, which prided itself in its citizens' loyalty, would let anyone depart from its borders. In addition, the road out of Russia led straight to Japan, an ally of Germany. Who would dare hope that the Japanese would allow these enemies of Hitler safe passage through their country? And anyway, how could transit visas through Japan possibly be obtained? The Japanese consul was in Riga, the capital of Latvia, and all travel from Vilna to Latvia was banned.

There then occurred another "coincidence" in this ongoing series of "accidental" developments.

In 1939, a Japanese commercial attache named Senpo Sugihara had suddenly arrived in nearby Kovno. No such consul had ever been posted in Kovno before, and Sugihara was to remain in the city for less than a year, until August, 1940. In fact, he had been dispatched there because the Japanese wanted him to report on possible German moves against Russia. In the meantime, though, he was to play a decisive role in the lives of thousands of Jews.

Seeking Japanese transit visas, several students called on the Japanese consulate in Kovno, only to find it shuttered. That appeared to obliterate their chances of escaping Vilna. Then, a short while later, while walking along the street, one of the Mirrer *talmidim* noticed an Oriental man beside him. What was an Oriental doing in Lithuania? Thinking fast, the student guessed that he had to be the Japanese consul. When the man was asked, he introduced himself as Mr. Sugihara and readily acknowledged his identity. Taking full advantage of the opportunity, the student asked if he could be issued a Japanese transit visa.

"It would be my pleasure, if that were possible," said Sugihara. "However, my government has just ordered me to close up the consulate and return to Japan. In fact, I have let my secretary go, and I am the only one left. So I do not think

I have the capability to help you."

So near, and yet so far? The *talmid* wouldn't give up. "If you need secretarial help, that's no problem. I have plenty of friends most willing to lend a hand. Only, we need those visas desperately. Without them, we are lost."

Sugihara didn't hesitate. "If you will help me out, then I have no objection at all. In fact, you can use my official stamp to validate the papers."

The *yeshivah* boys worked ferociously, under Sugihara's guidance. Despite their total unfamiliarity with Japanese, they helped prepare as many visas as possible. They found Sugihara most helpful and supportive. Even when his chiefs in Tokyo ordered him to stop issuing the visas, he ignored them. In fact, this act of insubordination subsequently led to his being fired. Eventually, some 3,500 Japanese transit visas were prepared, though not all were used. And Sugihara received not a penny of payment for his efforts. His motive was purely humanitarian.

DEALING WITH THE RUSSIANS

Some two thousand refugees made use of these Curacao end visas combined with Japanese transit visas. Of these, five hundred were *bnei yeshivah*, including the 250-member student body of the Mirrer Yeshivah and their *rebbeim*.

All their papers were now in order. Would the Russians agree to let them go? The students waited, and the answer was: Yes, but.

The papers were acceptable, and the students could travel across and out of Russia. However, when they applied for tickets for the Trans-Siberian Railroad, they found that the fare had suddenly skyrocketed from twenty dollars to one hudred and seventy dollars per person. That would require some fifty thousand dollars, an unthinkable amount, to cover the costs of the Mirrer *talmidim* alone. And the payment had to be made in American dollars. (The use of dollars was officially illegal in Russia, but the authorities looked the other way in eagerly accepting the coveted bills. One German-born student summoned the courage to complain to the German embassy about this requirement, and the German consul taunted the Russians: "What's the matter? Don't you accept your own currency?" As a result, this student alone was allowed to pay in Russian rubles.)

The *yeshivah* administrators tried to raise the required sum–equivalent to almost a million dollars today–but failed. The Joint Distribution Committee, which had supplied aid to the *talmidim* congregated in Lithuania, contributed five thousand dollars, but this was still far short of the goal. The Mirrer *roshei yeshivah* turned to one they knew would do anything to help. They dispatched an urgent message to Rabbi Kalmanowitz in America, simply stating, "Save us!"

When Rabbi Kalmanowitz received the plea, he needed no further prompting. Along with Irving Bunim, a successful businessman and an indefatigable community activist, he raced all over the New York Jewish community like a whirlwind, speaking to as many groups and individuals as possible. To each one, he warned of the tragic consequences that would arise if the money were not forthcoming. "Can we abandon the jewels of the glorious crown of Torah? Can we let these *yeshivah* students and their *rebbeim* be doomed to lives of captivity?"

His emotional appeals were most effective. Within a very short time, he raised forty thousand dollars on the *yeshivah's* behalf and secured loans for the remaining amount.

With the money now available, the Mirrer Yeshivah contingent was able to purchase the tickets and leave. They were among two thousand Polish refugees who traveled across Russia during early 1941. (There were other *yeshivah bachurim* in this number, but Mir was the only *yeshivah* that still had its student body intact.) Making the ten-day, six-thousand-mile trek across Siberia without incident, they arrived at the Pacific port of Vladivostok.

Unfortunately, not all the Polish refugees were able to use this escape route. They did not possess passports and were therefore denied permission to leave. Included in this group were *talmidim* from various *yeshivos*, such as Kamenitz, Kletz, Lubavitch and others. Their prospects suddenly brightened when, out of the blue, they received letters from Sweden granting them visas. Later, they learned that these had been sent by a German-born *bachur* named Shlomo Wolbe (later *mashgiach* of Yeshivas Be'er Yaakov in Eretz Yisrael). He had gone hungry and used his lunch money to purchase the visas.

Some were able to utilize these papers to leave Russia in time. Others, though, were less fortunate. Their applications for departure were delayed by bureaucratic red tape, and by the time they were due to receive permission, it was too late. Russia had banned further emigration.

As a result, the refugees, considered enemies of the state for their loyalty to *Yiddishkeit*, were rounded up and sent to Siberia. This was in mid-June, 1941. A week later, the Germans launched their surprise attack on Russia and quickly overran huge tracts of Soviet territory. Had the students not been brought to Siberia, they would have found themselves at the mercy of the Nazis. Not all survived the bitter Siberian experience, but almost none would have escaped the Nazi death warrant.

SAFE IN SHANGHAI

From Vladivostok, the Mirrer Yeshivah contingent moved on to the next available stop, which was Japan. Rickety ships, overcrowded and beset by storms, brought the refugees to the Japanese port of Kobe, where they arrived by March, 1941.

Some, such as Rabbi Aharon Kotler, *rosh yeshivah* of Kletzk, had by now received a visa to enter the United States, and they did so. But the majority could not get such visas. They had no intention of remaining in Japan for a lengthy time, but for now there was no other alternative. Their immediate concern was that their temporary transit visas would expire before they had found shelter elsewhere. What would the Japanese do to them if they did not move on before the deadline?

Once again, the unexpected occurred. The Japanese treated these strangers–so alien in custom and dress–with great courtesy and civility. And when their visas expired, they were renewed, again and again.

What accounted for this remarkable behavior from Hitler's cohorts? Oddly enough, part of the cause lay in the Nazis' anti-Jewish propaganda. One of Hitler's most outrageous canards was that the Jews were a powerful race with a disproportionate amount of influence plotting to take over the world. The Japanese came to accept it as fact. Giving weight to this belief was the Japanese memory of how the American Jewish financier Jacob Schiff had supplied huge loans that had enabled Japan to win the Russo-Japanese War in 1905.

Therefore, when these two thousand Jewish refugees arrived, the Japanese accorded them a respectful welcome. They thought that treating these Jews well would have a beneficial effect on their supposedly influential American brothers, who in turn would spread pro-Japanese feeling in the United States. (War between the two countries was still a year away.) Moreover, the Japanese hoped rich American Jews would lend them the billions of dollars needed to develop Manchuria, a part of China they had conquered. On the other hand, mistreating these Jews would create ill-will in America towards the Japanese. Taking no chances, the Japanese rejected Germany's vicious anti-Jewish policy.

The person who helped the refugees remain in Japan,

even though their transit visas of eight-to-fifteen days had long expired, was a unique individual named Professor Abraham Kotsuji. A Biblical scholar who took great interest in Jewish culture, Kotsuji was intrigued by these devout European Jews. Using his close connections to Japanese government officials, he was able to gain continued extension of the refugees' visas. After the war, he converted to Judaism and was honored by the Mirrer Yeshivah for his selfless help to the Jews during their hour of most dire need.

So the Jews stayed on in Kobe, as Rabbi Kalmanowitz and others relentlessly sought a means of transporting them elsewhere. In the meantime, the *talmidim* did not abandon their studies. If anything, the learning intensified, as the students realized that Torah was the key to their continued survival.

At the same time, the task of providing the *bnei yeshivah* with food and clothing was no small matter. The local Jewish community, aided by the Joint, provided some assistance, but these Orthodox Jews had special needs. Rabbi Kalmanowitz stepped up his campaign to maintain the *yeshivah*, shipping them both physical and spiritual necessities. He helped raise and then transferred large sums of money to Japan for the *yeshivah's* benefit.

As *Pesach* of 1941 approached, he secured the services of a boat to bring shipments of *matzoh* and wine to Kobe; they arrived just in time to assure that a traditional *seder* could be held. And at a time when *seforim* were far more expensive and less available than today, he sent them no fewer than two hundred copies of *Mesechte Kiddushin* to enable them to continue their studies properly.

The stay in Kobe came to an end shortly before *Rosh Hashanah* of 1941. The Japanese government ordered that the refugees be moved to Shanghai, an international city in the Japanese-controlled part of China. In Shanghai, they joined thousands of German refugees, as well as other Jews from around the world—including businessmen—who had established both Sephardic and Ashkenazic communities there.

The *bnei yeshivah* found accommodations in the impressive and spacious Beth Aharon Synagogue on Museum Road. The *shul* had been built as a bequest from a Jewish businessman in Shanghai but had rarely been used. Mr. D.E.J. Abraham, the Orthodox head of the Sephardic community in Shanghai, had made available this magnificent *shul* to the *yeshivah* as a *bais medrash*. Now the students moved in, to find that the structure had exactly enough room for them. It was as if the *shul* had been specifically erected to house them someday. Now its vast halls reverberated with the ringing rhythms of Torah learning.

Then, on December 7, 1941, Japanese planes launched their surprise attack on American bases in Pearl Harbor. A day later, Congress voted almost unanimously to declare war against Japan. Communications between the two nations were instantaneously severed.

These developments were especially ominous for the *bnei yeshivah*. Until then, they had subsisted mainly on funds sent from the United States. In addition to Rabbi Kalmanowitz's ongoing support, they had joined with other Shanghai Jews in getting aid from the Joint Distribution Committee in America. However, with Japan now an official enemy of the U.S., all such funds were legally cut off. How would the only *yeshivah* to survive intact keep the flame of Torah alive in this distant outpost?

A NEW AID ROUTE

Rabbi Kalmanowitz met the crisis not with despair but with stepped-up activism. The obstacles he faced were formidable. Since Japan was now America's hated enemy, trying to reach anyone there, including stranded Jews, was against the law. Even transmitting cables smacked of disloyalty, since perhaps the sender was a spy. The rules were quite strict, and as a result, the Joint had stopped dispatching funds for the Jewish refugees in Shanghai. For Rabbi Kalmanowitz, though, the case was not yet closed.

He organized meeting after meeting, establishing new contacts, and searching for new means to reach his beloved *talmidim*. Among those he linked up with at this time were Yitzchak and Recha Sternbuch of Switzerland, who had established their organization HIJEFS specifically to aid the Shanghai *bnei yeshivah*. Somehow, as a result of Rabbi Kalmanowitz's efforts, a complex, though illegal, arrangement was worked out whereby funds collected in the United States would reach the Jews of Shanghai via neutral countries like Switzerland. The Sternbuchs, as well as Hans Lehmann of Sweden, were instrumental in effecting this plan, and the United States eventually gave it its tacit approval. However, there were times when the government grew suspicious of Rabbi Kalmanowitz's activities. At one point, the FBI warned him that he was under their surveillance. That didn't slow him down one iota. "If I'm arrested," he said, "then if they let me out, I'll just do it again. The lives of the Jews in Shanghai are far more important than my comfort."

SURVIVING THE WAR AND BEYOND

The Mirrer Yeshivah remained based in Shanghai for five years, until 1946. During this time, the *talmidim* had to cope with the often unbearable heat and were stricken by illness due to vitamin deficiencies. Yet, they maintained their intensive learning schedule, even after the Shanghai Jewish community was relocated to a ghetto.

Fortunately, the Jewish ghetto in Shanghai, although overcrowded and unsanitary, was unlike its hellish counterparts in Nazi Europe. The inhabitants were allowed relative freedom, and for a year the *bnei yeshivah* were given permission to leave the ghetto during the day for their learning program. That program continued to thrive under the supervision of the Mirrer *rebbeim*, including Rabbi Yechezkel Lewenstein (who served as *mashgiach*) and especially the dynamic *rosh yeshivah* Rabbi Chaim Shmuelewitz, who provided his *talmidim* with the loving care of a devoted parent.

Even the lack of *sefarim* proved no deterrence. The *yeshivah* began printing its own volumes of sacred *sefarim*, with the help of Chinese lithographers who offset the texts brought to Shanghai by individuals. The first volume to be reprinted in this manner was *Mesechte Gittin*, and its completion in May, 1942, led to a public celebration in the Shanghai Jewish community. By 1946, close to one hundred *sefarim* had been published, including the entire *Tanach* and almost all of the Talmud.

During this five-year period, the *yeshivah* students were aided greatly by the hospitality shown by Rabbi Meir Ashkenazi, who had headed the Ashkenazic community of Shanghai since 1925. The students, in turn, aided the community by setting up a *yeshivah ketanah* to teach the children of their fellow refugees.

As the war's end neared, the *talmidim* experienced several close calls, due to American bombing of Shanghai and its surroundings. One student woke up in the middle of the night feeling ill and rushed to a doctor. When he returned, he found that the site where he had been sleeping had in the meantime been blown to bits by a bomb. There were a number of similar escapes, but not one of the *bnei yeshivah* was killed. The entire student body always remained gratefully aware of the obvious Hand of Hashem ensuring their survival.

On August 6, 1945, the United States dropped an atomic bomb on the Japanese city of Hiroshima, causing unprecedented loss of life and property. When a second bomb devastated Nagasaki, the Japanese Emperor signalled Japan's surrender. The war was over, but the Mirrer Yeshivah students were not yet "home."

The conclusion of the war was a time of great turmoil, especially for refugees. The transport of soldiers received highest priority, so arranging for the departure of Jews from Shanghai was very difficult indeed. Nevertheless, Rabbi Kalmanowitz succeeded. Using his numerous contacts in government, he pulled one string after another on the *yeshivah's* behalf. By 1946, the first group of students departed. The special arrangements for their departure prompted one Joint Distribution Committee representative to wonder, "Whom do they know in Washington to get them such service?"

By the beginning of 1948, all the Shanghai refugees had moved on, starting new lives elsewhere. The Mirrer Yeshivah, still intact, established branches in both Eretz Yisrael and in Brooklyn, New York, where they continue to thrive today. The *yeshiva's* incredible survival throughout the war was due in no small part to the dedication and *bitachon* of its *rebbeim* and *talmidim*, and to the unceasing efforts of Rabbi Kalmanowitz and his assistants to sustain them.

EXPANDED EFFORTS

Rabbi Kalmanowitz's activities to save the Mirrer *talmidim* led to his involvement with all aspects of *hatzalah* work during the war years. Along with Rabbi Aharon Kotler and Rabbi Eliezer Silver, he was a leader of the Vaad Hatzalah organization, set up specifically by the Orthodox community to rescue the *yeshivos* of Poland. But circumstances were to cause their small organizations to broaden its resue activities to include large masses of endangered Jews. Rabbi Kalmanowitz's credo was that any Jew, regardless of his background, must be saved, and that he would join with anyone, religious or not, in acts of rescue. His associates still remember seeing this rabbi in his black hat and long black *kapote* walking beside a bare-headed non-believer to raise money for the rescue cause.

His fund-raising abilities were legendary, and he never employed them more forcefully than during his campaigns for Vaad Hatzalah. In the early 1940s, the effects of the Depression still lingered, and people were reluctant to donate. Some also doubted that Europe's Jews were really in such dire peril.

However, the sweeping power of Rabbi Kalmanowitz's emotional pleas made them feel that they had no choice but to add their meager dollars to the collection. Vaad Hatzalah's appeals were essentially directed at the Orthodox Jewish community in America, whose members were poorer and older than their Reform or Conservative counterparts. Nevertheless, the organization was able to raise over a *million* dollars in 1944, an astounding total for those times and under those circumstances.

Rabbi Kalmanowitz's urgent appeals inspired others to perform similar acts of self-sacrifice.

When Rabbi Michoel Ber Weissmandl sent a cable desperately asking for funds to smuggle Jews out of Poland, Rabbi Kalmanowitz took up the cry. He set about delivering impassioned appeals to groups throughout the country, including the Associated Jewish Charities of Baltimore, Maryland. The audience included religious and non-religious leaders, and many of them felt that Rabbi Kalmanowitz was exaggerating the seriousness of the situation. However, the Orthodox rabbis present were so stirred by his words that they decided to take their own initiative rather than wait for the umbrella group to act.

One of them, Rabbi Shimon Schwab (later the *rav* of Khal Adath Jeshurun in the Washington Heights section of New York), made a special appeal to the members of Shearith

Israel, his congregation.

"This is the most important speech of my life," he began. "Now is hardly the time to live our lives as if everything is perfectly normal. We take freedom for granted; our European brothers and sisters can't. Therefore, we have to be truly generous, and ask more of ourselves than ever before. We cannot act like poor downtrodden people when so many others are living in horrible poverty and fear."

As Rabbi Schwab explained the situation facing European Jews, his congregants resolved to do everything possible on their behalf. They were not wealthy, but they gave whatever they could. Many of the women donated their personal jewelry to aid the rescue effort.

Then Rabbi Schwab rose to announce his own contribution. "I am just a poor refugee myself, having arrived here not too long ago from Germany. I, therefore, do not have many resources. But I do have one treasure I cherish above anything else, a *Sefer Torah* entrusted to me after the Nazis closed my *shul* in Germany.

"There are only three instances in which one is permitted to sell a *Sefer Torah*. One of these comes when someone's life is in danger. Certainly what we face today is a matter of *hatzalas nefashos*. Therefore, I am offering this personal treasure for sale, as my contribution to the rescue appeal."

One of the trustees of the *shul* purchased the Torah for the sum of one thousand dollars. (The dollar then was worth several times its present value.) However, instead of keeping it, he placed it in the *aron hakodesh* to be used by the *tzibbur*. This donation helped the members raise the very considerable total of ten thousand dollars for the rescue of Polish Jews.

SHATTERING NEWS

The full extent of the Nazi treachery became clear to

Rabbi Kalmanowitz on September 3, 1942. That day, he received a tragic phone call from his colleague Yitzchak Sternbuch in Switzerland.

"It's true," Sternbuch reported mournfully. "All the rumors. It's happened. Hundreds of thousands have already died. There may be over a million." He was sobbing.

"But how do you know?" asked Rabbi Kalmanowitz. "How can you be sure?"

"A Polish Jew managed to escape from a Nazi death camp. He's given us a full report. He went through it; he's seen it all."

Rabbi Kalmanowitz listened numbly as Mr. Sternbuch recounted the eyewitness account, confirming the worst and more.

His secretary Rabbi Alex Weisfogel, in an adjourning room heard an unearthly cry, and then a crashing thud.

He rushed inside, and found Rabbi Kalmanowitz lying prone on the floor, the phone receiver still in his hand. The astounding news had made him faint dead away.

Rabbi Weisfogel picked up the phone and heard Sternbuch repeat the message. After he put down the phone, Rabbi Weisfogel spoke to the revived Rav Kalmanowitz. Still trembling, he vowed to take immediate action. The world had to be alerted to the incredible truth and finally do something to stop further killings.

PRESSURING THE GOVERNMENT

Rabbi Kalmanowitz and Yaakov Rosenheim, head of World Agudah saw the clear need to initiate diplomatic moves of their own. To that end, as soon as he obtained a copy of the Sternbuch cable, Moreinu Rosenheim sent an urgent cable to President Roosevelt, requesting an emergency meeting. The cable was never answered.

On the other hand, Rabbi Kalmanowitz and other Jewish leaders did get to meet with Treasury Secretary Henry Morgenthau, himself a Jew. Morgenthau was personally a totally assimilated Jew, but Rabbi Kalmanowitz's powerful impact made a dramatic impression on him. As a result, Morgenthau called Secretary of State Cordell Hull, a man with no special interest in saving Jews, and asked him to raise the issue of Jewish suffering with the President.

Word came back from Hull: "Sorry. I have no time."

Morgenthau grew furious. "In all these years I've never asked for anything on behalf of my people. If I can't get the President's ear now, then I might as well quit."

This uncharacteristic outburst came to Roosevelt's attention, and he agreed to the meeting. As a result, on December 8 he met with five representatives of American Jewry, including Rabbi Rosenberg of the Union of Orthodox Rabbis. On December 17, 1942, the Allies issued the only declaration they ever put out during the war that condemned Nazi crimes against the Jews and promised eventual punishment for the perpetrators. This established the basis for the Nuremberg Trials that brought Nazi leaders to justice after the war.

Getting the American government to intercede on behalf of European Jews was no easy matter. Although Roosevelt had several Jewish aides, he lacked the courage and resolve to counter American anti-Jewish prejudice by actively aiding Europe's Jews. In addition, some government officials, notably. Assistant Secretary of State Breckinridge Long, were anti-Jewish at heart and blocked all measures designed to help Jews. Finally, some American Jewish leaders downplayed the question of Jewish suffering to avoid making the war a Jewish issue and thereby stir up more anti-Jewish feeling.

Nevertheless, there were Jewish leaders (both Orthodox and non-Orthodox) who kept urging their government contacts to take bold steps to save Jews. When Rabbi Kalmanowitz heard from Rabbi Weissmandl of the need to raise funds for

Hungarian and Slovakian Jews, or to make the Allies bomb Auschwitz, he pushed these contacts relentlessly for action.

His assistant Rabbi Alex Weisfogel grew accustomed to being summoned by Rabbi Kalmanowitz at all hours of the day or night. It was therefore not at all unexpected when Rabbi Weisfogel's phone rang at three o'clock one morning and he heard the familiar voice on the other end bubbling with urgency and excitement, "I have some new ideas on our latest *hatzalah* project, and I need you to come with me to the Labor Department in Philadelphia. Can you be ready to meet me at Penn Station in four hours?" When action was imperative, sleep could wait.

One Friday in 1941, a group of volunteers gathered in a room, carefully compiling a list of potential refugees from Europe. Rabbi Kalmanowitz was with them, supervising their efforts and constantly reminding them to copy the information accurately. "That is extremely important," he kept saying. "The names you are writing down are those of our poor brothers and sisters overseas. Since many of them have relatives here in America, there is a chance that we can get them emergency visitor visas. Every Jew we save from the Nazis, *yemach shemam*, is a victory for us. But for this to happen, we have to make sure the Justice Department gets the list in proper form and on time."

Next to him, assisting in the work as usual, was Rabbi Weisfogel. As he paused from his list-making chores, Rabbi Weisfogel noticed the first fiery embers of sunset on the horizon.

"Shabbos is coming," he announced. "We'll have to stop here. Can any of you come back on *Motzei Shabbos* to finish the job?"

Before anyone could respond, Rabbi Kalmanowitz went to the phone, dialed a number and conducted a short but intense conversation with another party. As he hung up, he sighed deeply and then turned to the others in the room.

"I just spoke to the Justice Department office in Philadelphia. They said they cannot wait for the list much longer. If they are going to act on it, they need it by tomorrow!"

"But that's impossible," someone said. "The lists aren't finished yet."

"I do not know the meaning of that word impossible," Rabbi Kalmanowitz countered. "We will have the lists finished and on the desk of the Justice Department offices by tomorrow morning, as required."

"But *Shabbos*!" The puzzlement showed on the faces of many in the room.

"Believe me, I know it is almost *Shabbos*. But when it comes to *pikuach nefesh*, it is commanded that you work until the person is saved. This overrides every other rule in the Torah, even *Shabbos*. So there is no question that we can–we must–continue our job here until it is done."

The work continued until well past midnight. But it was indeed completed, and the list did wind up on the Justice Department desk before the deadline. Most important, a number of those whose names were on it were eventually saved.

Before the bone-weary volunteers departed, Rabbi Kalmanowitz shared a last thought with them. "Believe me, my friends, no one missed the special *Shabbos* rest, the special *Shabbos* spirit, tonight more than I. What I wouldn't have given to have been at home with my family, sitting at the *Shabbos* table and singing *zemiros*. But sometimes we must make sacrifices. And to enable even one Jew to come to these shores and celebrate *Shabbos* in freedom . . . for that, my friends, any sacrifice is worthwhile."

THE CONGRESSMAN CHANGES HIS MIND

Rabbi Kalmanowitz became a familiar figure in high government offices. One of those he met with often was Congressman Emanuel Celler, who represented parts of Brooklyn, New York.

Later, Congressman Celler recalled his first view of Rabbi Kalmanowitz, looking like a patriarch, with his long black coat and cloud-white beard, leaning on a cane, seeming aged and feeble, with tears streaming down his cheeks.

"Can't you understand," he told the Congressman, "that there are millions–millions!–being killed? We have to save them. Isn't there something you can do to help, Mr. Celler?"

Congressman Celler tried to explain to this old rabbi that he had been in touch with the President about the problem but that the bureaucratic wheels of government turned very slowly. The rabbi had to be patient.

All of a sudden, the old rabbi became an angry, energetic firebrand. Pounding his cane on the floor, he demanded, "If six million *cattle* had been slaughtered, there would have been greater concern! A way would have been found to protect them. But these are people. People! And they must be saved."

That night, Congressman Celler had a haunting dream. He saw an ancient rabbi with a flowing white beard standing on a rock in the ocean and groups of people trying to make their way through the water to get to the rock. He then saw the people turn into cattle and then back into humans. Finally, he saw himself on the shore, held back by a rope which someone was pulling. When he awoke, he realized his lack of action was gnawing on his conscience.

From that point on, Congressman Celler resolved to switch his approach, and he became quite aggressive in fighting the government red tape holding up refugee aid. In addition, Congressman Celler played the key role in getting the Shanghai Jews to the United States as quickly as possible after the war.

SWAYING THE TREASURY SECRETARY

Another government official whom Rabbi Kalmanowitz spurred to action was Treasury Secretary Henry Morgenthau. As mentioned earlier, Morgenthau was an assimilated Jew whose links to his heritage were weak. He was at first not inclined to exert his influence on behalf of Jewish issues. However, his meetings with Rabbi Kalmanowitz and other Jewish leaders altered his attitude.

One such meeting, occurring after the one described above, took place in the spring of 1944. At that time, some Jews still alive in Nazi-occupied lands owed their continued survival to Latin American papers. These papers had been provided to them by George Mantello, the Sternbuchs and others. Jews who held them were accorded respectful treatment by the Nazis, because they wanted good treatment for the thousands of Germans living in Latin America. Then word spread that the Latin American countries that had earlier backed up these papers were no longer willing to do so. As a result, the Jews holding them would become prime targets for deportation.

Recha Sternbuch quickly contacted Rabbis Kalmanowitz and Rosenheim in America and implored them to remedy the situation. She suggested they ask the U.S. State Department to pressure the Latin American countries to recognize the papers officially.

The *rabbonim* and their associates quickly arranged a conference with one of President Roosevelt's Jewish advisors, and he promised to contact the State Department–but never did so. So on Pesach they travelled to Washington, to try to save Jewish lives. They went to Morgenthau, and Rabbi Kalmanowitz acted as their spokesmen. In his broken English, he delivered an impassioned plea for immediate help. Telling of the plight of those with the papers, he concluded with the words, "Please, Mr. Secretary, do the very most you can do to save them."

After that, Morgenthau recorded later, the rabbis began to weep, unable to contain their anguish over their fellow Jews. Rabbi Kalmanowitz was not one to hide his emotions, and he would often cry in public when he pleaded the refugees' cause.

The normally cool and unemotional Morgenthau was obviously shaken by the encounter. He decided to bypass the usual governmental channels and apply direct pressure on the State Department. He called Secretary of State Hull directly but was again told that the Secretary was busy.

"Then I'll hold on until he's free," he said with sudden determination.

He finally did get through, and after some arm-twisting, the all-important cables to the Latin American countries were at last dispatched.

Morgenthau was pleased. "We finally got something done," he told his staff. "And if some of those in the government don't like the way I've pushed this through and are calling me a dirty Jew . . . well, that's just too bad."

THE RABBIS MARCH ON WASHINGTON

Sometimes, the heads of Vaad Hatzalah felt that public displays of concern were necessary, both to arouse public and governmental interest and to demonstrate that European Jewry had not been forgotten.

At first, the Orthodox leaders hoped that a united front of all American Jewish groups—Orthodox and non-Orthodox—would provide the best possible image of Jewish concern over their brothers' fate. However, when non-religious leaders indicated that they would use the rally to showcase their own priorities, the Orthodox decided to chart their own approach.

Thus, four hundred Orthodox rabbis joined in the initiative of Peter Bergson to stage a march in Washington, D.C., on behalf of European Jewry. Bergson was a leader of the Revisionist Zionists, who differed fundamentally from the Socialist Zionists in their views towards Jewish emigration to Eretz Yisrael. The Socialist Zionists wanted to establish a Jewish State dominated by strong young *chalutzim* (pioneers) dedicated to the socialism rather than to Judaism. They disdained the image of the bearded, religious *shtetl* Jew and gave low priority to rescuing European Jewry. The Revisionist Zionists, on the other hand, were interested in having *all* Jews settle in Eretz Yisrael and thus were very concerned with rescuing European Jewry, including the religious segment.

Bergson (a nephew of former Chief Rabbi Avraham Kook) was a master at using public relations to draw attention to the plight of European Jewry. He ran dramatic ads written by noted author Ben Hecht in newspapers and staged a stirring rally in Madison Square Garden. All this earned him the disdain of the secular Jewish establishment in America, whose leaders wanted to prevent the war from becoming a Jewish issue.

Nevertheless, Bergson persisted, and came up with the idea of the march on Washington. It was warmly endorsed by the leaders of the Vaad Hatzalah, especially Rabbi Eliezer Silver. Rabbi Silver took the lead in getting other *rabbonim*, including Rabbi Kalmanowitz, to attend.

The date for the march was very symbolic: the day before *Erev Yom Kippur*, 1943—during the *Aseres Yemei Teshuvah*, with the Day of Judgment approaching. It would be a clear call for the free world to display its conscience.

Many of the irreligious leaders scoffed at the notion of such a public demonstration, worried that it might bring unwanted attention to American Jewish demands. A number of President Roosevelt's "Jewish" advisors persuaded him not to meet with the group, claiming they were not representative of American Jewry as a whole.

Nevertheless, the *rabbonim* insisted on going forward with the march, and it proceeded right on schedule. Though they would normally be the last ones to demonstrate publicly, and they certainly were busy enough at home right before *Yom Kippur*, they could not remain silent bystanders while the European tragedy was unfolding. Continued silence would turn them into virtual co-conspirators with their people's murderers. If a march would capture Washington's attention, then it was necessary.

Therefore, on October 6, 1943, the nation's capital witnessed a most unusual scene, as four hundred traditionally-dressed *rabbonim*, with Rabbis Silver and Kalmanowitz prominently among them, walked as a group from the Capitol building to the White House. Even jaded government officials, who had viewed many demonstrations in their day, took note of the event. Though the President had heeded his advisors' warnings and stayed away, Vice President Henry Wallace, House Speaker Sam Rayburn and other officials did meet with the *rabbonim* and heard their calls for action.

Most important, the march eventually helped lead to concrete results. It was a major factor in prompting Congressional hearings on a proposal for a government agency to rescue Jews. Secretary Morgenthau played a decisive role in pressuring the President to create such an agency. He and his staff submitted a report entitled "The American Government's Acquiescence in the Murder of Europe's Jews." This accused State Department officials (especially Assistant Secretary of State Breckinridge Long) of sabotaging all attempts to save Jews from the Nazis.

Roosevelt, entering an election year, at last took action. On January 22, 1944, he created the War Refugee Board, charged with coming to the aid of Hitler's designated victims (most of whom were, by now, dead). Although the Board's final effect was limited, it was still the only government body that attempted a sustained effort to help European Jews during the war. It is estimated that the War Refugee Board, in conjunction with the various Jewish rescue activists throughout the free world, managed to save more than two hundred thousand Jewish lives.

The director of the Board was John Pehle, a non-Jew. He, too, came to respect Rabbi Kalmanowitz's dedication to his fellow Jews. They met many times, and Pehle learned from him how important it was not to procrastinate when lives hung in the balance.

Once Rabbi Kalmanowitz came to Washington to see Pehle about an issue that required an immediate response. The hour grew late, and Pehle was about to leave with the matter still unresolved.

"Don't worry, rabbi," he said, "I'll speak to Secretary Morgenthau about this first thing in the morning. Now I'm afraid I have to be going home. In the meantime, why don't you sleep on it?"

"Sleep on it?" exclaimed Rabbi Kalmanowitz. "How can I possibly sleep at a time like this? I'll just wait here until morning." Then he took a seat in Pehle's office and opened a *sefer* he had brought along.

Pehle didn't know what to do. Finally, in as gentle a tone as he could muster, he said, "But rabbi, if you stay, you'll be disturbing the cleaning women."

"Don't worry," was the reply. "I'll keep out of their way." Then he returned to his learning, clearly prepared to remain till dawn.

Pehle realized that this matter was an emergency and could not be confined to the normal business hours.

"All right, rabbi," he said. "You win. Let's go to Mr. Morgenthau right now and take care of everything so that we can all have a good night's sleep."

THE SURVIVING LEGACY

Though he bitterly grieved over those he could not save, Rabbi Kalmanowitz was overjoyed when Jewish survivors emerged from Europe, especially his beloved colleagues and *talmidim* of the Mirrer Yeshivah. He remained committed to serving the *yeshivah* and was intimately associated with it until his death in 1965.

For his tireless work on behalf of Jews throughout the world, Rabbi Kalmanowitz was the worthy recipient of the undying gratitude of all Jews. But it was perhaps a non-Jew, John Pehle, who best spoke for all those who had known the sage. At a dinner tendered by the Mirrer Yeshivah to honor Pehle and Secretary Morgenthau after the war, he remarked: "No one in government, or out of it, was more devoted to our lifesaving mission than Rabbi Kalmanowitz. His hard work, his earnestness and his enduring faith were an ever-present inspiration to us all."

A HOME FOR THE HOMELESS

REB ELIMELECH ("MIKE") TRESS

Reb Elimelech ("Mike") Tress, architect of American Zeirei
and Agudath Israel, was one of the earliest and most effective
rescue activists. He helped hundreds of endangered Jews gain
entry to the United States before the war, including Rav Aaron
Kotler and scores of *roshei yeshivah* and *yeshivah* students,
helping them adjust upon their arrival. He also became very
influential in Washington during numerous rescue efforts.

3   A HOME FOR THE HOMELESS

REB ELIMELECH ("MIKE") TRESS

THE BEDRAGGLED IMMIGRANT GRASPED THE PIECE OF PAPER AS if it were a lifeline. By now, it was smudged and tattered, but the address on it was still clearly visible: 616 Bedford Avenue in a place called Williamsburg, Brooklyn. A fellow newcomer to America had handed it to him, along with the assurance, "Go there. They'll treat you right."

He wondered. How could he look forward to anyone's help anymore? How, for that matter, could he trust anyone at all? Not after all he'd been through. Not after all the inhumanity he'd witnessed. Not after all the horrors he'd seen.

Somehow, he'd managed to escape that last round-up of Jews and flee to safety. Some safety. How could he feel the least bit secure when he was always on the run, looking over his shoulder for the threat that lurked forever behind him? And when he'd finally managed to sneak out of the Nazis' shadow, he'd still been at a loss. Where was he to go now? What country was willing to take him?

Fortunately, he had a relative in the United States who'd

supplied him with an all-important affidavit. That made him one of the privileged few who were able to scurry across the Atlantic Ocean to gain America's unenthusiastic welcome. But now what was he to do? The relative didn't want to hear further from him; he'd spent too much on him already. So there he was, alone in a mammoth new foreign country, his family torn from him, his memories tormented by terrors, his future bleak. He had no home, no job, no knowledge of the language. Would all his tomorrow's be as hopeless as his yesterdays? Had he escaped Mitzrayim only to die in the Midbar?

He'd been told to meet with a representative of a Jewish organization he'd never heard of. But the meeting hadn't gone well. The man interviewing him could converse with him in Yiddish, but he really didn't speak his language. The interviewer seemed to lack sympathy for a Jew who'd sacrificed so much to keep his *Yiddishkeit* alive while death was everywhere. There was a chilly, formal atmosphere to the encounter, as if the interviewer were talking to just another statistic. It hadn't made the newcomer feel at home in the least.

Then this second suggestion had come, to visit the address in Williamsburg. "Go there and ask for a man named Tress," he'd been told. "He'll know how to take care of you." Probably another starch-shirted bureaucrat. But he'd gone anyway. What did he have to lose?

It had taken him some time in this hurly-burly city to find the right place. The building seemed smaller than some of the others he'd been to, but an aura of purposeful activity pervaded it. People, many of them clearly religious Jews, kept entering and leaving. There was movement here; something important was happening. It seemed encouraging.

He entered, dreading the presence of a solemn secretary who would direct him to a seat and load him down with impossible forms to fill out. Instead, he came face to face with a young, vigorous man in shirtsleeves.

"Shalom aleichem! Vos macht a Yid?" the man boomed out in affectionate greeting. "With whom do I have the pleasure of speaking?"

"My name is Fried. Chaim Fried. I arrived here just a few days ago."

"Just arrived? Well, where are you staying? Do you have enough to eat? Have you found a *minyan* yet?"

"I . . . um . . . thank you for asking. But I was told to speak to a Mr. Tress. I suppose he's very busy, though."

"He is, but he'll be more than happy to meet you." The employee grinned. "In fact, you've already met him, and you're now looking him in the face. But please, whatever you do, don't be so formal. Never call me Mr. Tress. I'm simply Mike. And I know you've had a hard journey getting here, in more ways than one. So why don't we sit down over here, and you'll tell me all the ways we can help you."

Within minutes, the forlorn wanderer had gained a place to stay, free of charge. And for the first time in months, he could stop running and rebuild his life.

This *heimishe* hospitality came from an American-born dynamo in his early thirties. He was one of a new breed of American Jews who were not ashamed to show off their allegiance to Torah.

Elimelech "Mike" Tress was a typical American go-getter, but what he pursued was the chance to save his endangered European brothers. As the driving force behind Zeirei Agudath Israel of America before and during the war years, he harnessed the talents of young Americans like himself to help bring over a steady flow of desperate refugees. Through his unrelenting efforts, thousands of Jews like Chaim Fried were able to make the adjustment to a meaningful life in America. Although they were short on funds and manpower, these youthful rescue workers were often able to accomplish what organizations with budgets that overwhelmed theirs couldn't.

BROOKLYN BORN AND BRED

Unlike the other personalities depicted in this volume, Elimelech Tress was a native-born American. He hailed from the Williamsburg section of Brooklyn, where he was born in 1909. At the time, the United States was popularly considered a spiritual wasteland among the Orthodox Jews of Europe, and for good reason.

The American penchant for independence and the pursuit of riches did not seem compatible with Torah Judaism's emphasis on tradition and altruism. The future appeared to lie with Reform and its credo: "Be a Jew at home, but an American in public." Jews who stood out were scorned. In this atmosphere, it was not surprising that, at that time, *yeshivos* were few.

As a boy, Elimelech Tress never attended a *yeshivah*. Like many other religious Jews of his day, he received his secular education in public school and his religious upbringing at home and at a Talmud Torah. This training was complicated by the fact that his father died when he was quite young. After attending college, he sought a career in business and became, to all outward appearances, a typical American success story—a manager in the Lamport Textile Factory and an outgoing, personable man who liked to be called Mike.

It would have been easy for him to forfeit his roots in the American melting pot. That never happened, though. The example of his family's religious observance was one reason. The inspiration offered by European-born *rabbonim* was certainly another.

Joining the nearby *minyan* of the Stoliner Rebbe, where his widowed mother prayed, the young Tress was drawn to the Rebbe's warmth and commitment to the welfare of the *klal*. From the Rebbe, he learned both the intricacies of the Torah and how to actively address the needs of his fellow Jews.

A secretary was required at the Lamport firm, and Mike Tress was in a position to choose one. Among the applicants was a young lady from a religious immigrant family.

One of the other bosses was skeptical. "I don't think a greenhorn would fit in here."

Tress thought otherwise and hired her. She was grateful for the chance.

"If I hadn't gotten this job," she said, "I would have had to take another one that would have forced me to come in on *Shabbos*."

"That won't happen here," Tress assured her. "As long as I have some say about it, you'll never have a problem staying a *Shabbos* observer at this firm."

The secretary was the first of many young women who were able to escape poverty yet remain *frum*, due to Mike Tress's intervention. This policy brought him personal benefit, too. One of the women he hired eventually became his wife.

ACTIVISM THROUGH AGUDAH

Encouraged by the Stoliner Rebbe and members of his *minyan* who belonged to Zerei, Tress joined them, soon rising to become president. Tress sought to expand his *klal* work by helping run youth groups under the auspices of Zerei. A partnership that was eventually to change his life and preserve the lives of countless others as well.

Agudath Israel was a vision of *achdus* initiated at the behest of the foremost *gedolim* of Europe. In 1912, representatives of Torah communities in both Eastern and Western Europe met in Katowitz, Poland, to inaugurate the organization. Guided by such luminaries as Rabbi Chaim Ozer Grodzinski, the Chafetz Chaim and the Gerrer Rebbe, among many others, Agudath Israel promoted many programs that protected Orthodox interests and strengthened Torah learning. Its central goal was to battle the assimilation threatening the Jewish world.

In America, though, the Agudah remained a relatively minor force on the Jewish scene through the early 1930s, for reasons mentioned earlier. It was mainly in evidence through the Zeirei, its organization for young Orthodox adults. Elimelech Tress and his fellow activists helped bring about a major turnaround in the fortunes of both the Zeirei and the American Agudah itself.

Tress did not join Zeirei Agudath Israel to seek glory or satisfy political ambitions. Rather, he was concerned at first with improving *Yiddishkeit* among the youth. Along with others his age, Tress reached out to the multitudes of irreligious Jewish youth in the neighborhood and organized gatherings that introduced these products of Jewish apathy to the warmth and fulfillment that flow from true *Yiddishkeit*. And they ran weekly Pirchei groups for Jewish youngsters to keep them constructively occupied on *Shabbos* and other occasions.

At the same time, these Zeirim who could inspire others could themselves be inspired by the *gedolim*.

In 1937, the renowned Rabbi Elchonon Wasserman, *rosh yeshivah* in Baranovitch, Poland, arrived in the United States for what would prove to be a two-year stay. His primary goal was to obtain desperately-needed funds for his *yeshivah*. At the same time, Rabbi Chaim Ozer Grodzinski had urged him to make the journey to help strengthen the struggling Torah communities in America. In his public and private meetings throughout the country, Reb Elchonon did just that. The force of his saintly personality and the abundant evidence of his profound scholarship made a singular impression on his audience. Of all those who met him, none was more influenced than Elimelech Tress.

Reb Elchonon's encounters with the members of Zeirei

Agudath Israel, to whom he imparted *Divrei Torah* and philosophical insights in many *shiurim* and *mussar shmuzzen*, were truly historic. Here was an acclaimed giant of European *limud* encountering young American-born Jews and establishing a dynamic bond with them. It was a chance for both parties to discover the strengths of the other and to find if they could work together towards a common purpose. For Elimelech Tress in particular, it proved he could be a fully-acknowledged link in the chain of Jewish tradition. An American public school product could continue the holy work of his European ancestors. His talks with Reb Elchonon convinced Tress to abandon his business career and devote himself full-time to *klal* work. This, insisted Reb Elchonon, was what Hashem meant for Tress to do.

This personal decision met the tide of history at a most turbulent time. Reb Elchonon returned to Europe (where he would eventually perish) just before the outbreak of war in 1939. When the Zeirei members came to see Reb Elchonon off, the sage turned to Elimelech Tress and told him, "The future of Torah in America is in your hands."

IN PURSUIT OF AFFIDAVITS

The reports of the savagery of Kristallnacht in Germany and Austria in November, 1938, rocked the American Jewish community. There had, of course, been earlier accounts of the Nazis' brutality. Hoping against hope, some Jews had earlier tried to downplay the threat to their European brethren. Now, however, there was no denying its virulence. Some responded with angry words or despondent sighs. Then there were those who sought to take action.

By this time, a sizable group of Zeirei activists had emerged. Some, like Meir Shenkolewski, Gershon Kranzler, Moishe Berger and Charles Richter, had emigrated from

Europe. Others were native-born Americans. Whatever their origins, they turned instinctively to Mike Tress for direction. His vibrance and resoluteness, his talent for dynamic speech-making, his ability to relate well to the American scene, all made him a natural leader for the times. And the times called for immediate expressions of *achdus* with the beleaguered Jews of Europe.

At the same time, Tress learned from these immigrants' talents and drive. He gained insight through their knowledge of European traditions, as well as their familiarity with the philosophy of the European Agudah.

War had not yet broken out in late 1938. Nevertheless, after Kristallnacht, Tress foresaw years of anguish and suffering for his fellow Jews around the world. So although he was feeling ill that day, he summoned his closest Zeirei *chaverim* to an emergency meeting in his aunt's house. In a tiny, crowded room, they listened in hushed wonder as he spoke.

"*Rabbosai*, we've worked together, all of us, to build some wonderful programs for young Jews living around us. These must continue and even grow. But for now, our sights have to turn across the ocean. Jews are being attacked there. Holy, saintly *Yiddin, Yiddin* who have been our leaders and our inspiration. We have to come to their aid immediately!"

A murmur arose among the group. True, action was needed. But what could a few individuals in their teens and twenties do to combat events thousands of miles away?

"Why do we always have to think of our limitations?" Mike countered. "Why don't we think of our strengths? We're young, we've got energy, and we're working for the most important cause in the world–saving human lives. With Hashem's help, there's nothing we can't do."

With that, he began to outline a concrete plan for action. It was ambitious but rooted firmly in reality.

Jews who faced danger in Europe had to be delivered to safety whenever possible. Bringing them to America was difficult, they knew. The immigration laws were strict. Americans didn't want foreigners, especially Jews, streaming over their borders. Yet, there were indeed ways of gaining permission for Jews to enter the United States. These had to be pursued at all deliberate speed.

One way the United States had limited immigration was by setting tight quotas on how many immigrants could enter from each of the various countries around the world. Even if slots were available within the quota, immigrants had to get an affidavit from a relative or friend in America before being allowed to enter. The affidavit was a signed document stating that the relative or friend was willing to support the refugee and prevent his becoming a financial burden on the public. Without this moral guarantee, potential immigrants, even those fleeing a mortal enemy, could see their dreams of becoming Americans fade into despair.

Affidavits, then, were essential. European Jews were begging Jewish groups to help provide them. Perhaps the Zeirim could go out and actively secure these papers. It was certainly worth a try. Influential people had to be approached and contacts built. The more affidavits, the more Jews could be brought over.

There were other approaches to consider, too. Those Jews still stranded in Europe had to be sent aid and encouragement to remain alive for later possible rescue. And the incoming refugees had to be welcomed and cared for, so they could rebuild their lives in a jarring new environment.

Could all this be accomplished by a group of young political novices?

"These may seem like dreams, *rabbosai*," Tress concluded. "But if we just sit here saying nothing can be done, then that's just what will happen. Nothing."

The others listened with growing resolve and admiration. None were more impressed than the European-born members of the group. Here, indeed, was someone with the

127

industriousness of an American but the unselfish devotion of a universal Jew.

What the group didn't at first anticipate was just how tangled the red tape that awaited them could be. Securing government approval of even minor requests often required complex paperwork and tormenting delays. Fortunately, Agudah member Meir Shenkolewski had already done this type of work for Rabbi Dr. Leo Jung, a noted rabbinical leader and a veteran of dealing with official requirements for immigrants. With the help of both Rabbi Dr. Jung, and the remarkable Rabbi Eliezer Silver of Cincinnati, who helped them raise funds for the task, the young activists continued to gain experience in filling out the required forms. Slowly, they wended their way through the maze of bureaucratic rules.

Their growing expertise soon began paying off. They started helping families bring over European relatives, assisting them with the necessary forms and seeking new ways of securing immigration. They were among the first to obtain Paraguayan passports for Jews without other exit papers. And sometimes they took quick, ingenious action that made all the difference between life and death.

Charles Richter, a young Agudah activist living in Vienna, Austria, was named by Tress to serve as the official contact in Vienna of Zeirei's Refugee and Immigration Division. After Kristallnacht, a Viennese Jew approached him about the prospect of immigrating with his family to the United States.

"Where were you born?" Richter asked.

"In a small town in Rumania."

"That's not good. The American quota for Rumanians is very small, and it's already used up for this year."

With his life at stake, the man wouldn't give up. "Isn't there anything you can do?"

Richter mulled over the situation. "Well . . . Rumania might be out, but the Russian quota isn't filled yet. Anyone born in Russia probably has a good chance of being admitted."

The man was puzzled. "But what good does that do me? I come from Rumania, not Russia."

"Yes, but you were born in a small town there. If you list it, no one will know it's in Rumania. Why don't you say it's in Russia instead?"

"But is that legal?"

"We're talking about saving your life!"

The man followed Richter's clever advice, and he and his family made it safely to America.

Sometimes, good ideas were just the initial step to success. As the members of Zeirei learned to their dismay, getting even relatives to sign affidavits for their European brethren was often problematic.

"But doesn't this obligate me to support them for years and years?" they worried. "That will cost me thousands!"

Of course, at the time, most American Jews had no idea just how horrendous the final fate of Europe's Jews would be.

The members of Zeirei had a clearer picture of the truth. Many of them were European refugees themselves. As more and more of them arrived in the United States, they were able to supply first-hand accounts of the true nature of the European Jews' plight. Rabbi Gedaliah Schorr, later *rosh yeshivah* in Torah Vodaath, was an American *yeshivah bachur* who had learned in the Kletsk Yeshivah under Rabbi Aharon Kotler in 1938-9. He returned right before war broke out with a message of urgency from Reb Aharon: "Every Jew who isn't brought out of Europe now is as good as dead."

Zeirei was put on an emergency footing. Results had to be attained, regardless of the cost. If relatives were afraid affidavits would prove too costly, then Zeirei would underwrite the obligation. Copies still exist of letters written by Mike Tress and his colleagues, guaranteeing full financial backing to those who would not otherwise have issued affidavits. To meet these obligations, Tress and his co-workers wrote hundreds of letters and spent hours meeting with wealthy individuals to raise money for these ventures.

Among these was an enormously wealthy Jew who had earned a fortune in real estate. Unfortunately, he was also notorious for rejecting out of hand all requests for charity. At a time when the Zeirei's bankroll was minuscule, and affidavits were growing scarce, a Zeirei activist named Moishe Berger (head of its Refugee and Immigration Division) decided to approach this skinflint. What, he figured, did he have to lose?

His first attempts at contacting the man met with resounding failure. The tycoon's secretary adamantly refused to put Berger's call through to her boss. Berger then worked hard to locate the man's residence and finally phoned him at his home in Brooklyn.

"Hello, I am calling for the Immigration Division . . ." He paused and then adopted a much lower tone. " . . . of Zeirei."

The businessman heard only the key words. "Yes, of course. You want to meet with me. My pleasure. How about tomorrow at ten in the morning?"

When Berger arrived for his appointment, the secretary threw him a withering stare.

"How often do I have to tell you he will *never* have time for you?"

"But I'm scheduled to meet with him today at ten."

"Impossible."

"Well," said Berger, "why don't you go in to him and check?"

The secretary, marching in confidently, did just that. She emerged a deflated woman. "He says to go right in."

Berger did so, to find a small man sitting behind a mammoth desk, blowing cigar smoke to the ceiling. Not giving him a chance to speak, Berger launched into a tear-filled plea on behalf of the embattled Jews of Europe.

"I know just how threatened these Jews are," he said. "I've only recently escaped from Europe myself. And if wealthy

Jews like you don't use your money to help save them, what good is it all? It's just for emergencies like these that Heaven grants some Jews great wealth. Now here's your chance to use it on behalf of others. Don't you see?"

When the pitch was over, Berger looked up to see the tycoon gazing at him, puffing steadily on the cigar.

"Young man," he finally said. "What's your name?"

Berger told him. He figured the man would report him to the Immigration Office for false impersonation. But at this point, he no longer cared.

The tycoon let the smoke swirl over his head. "You know, Berger, I've been working hard to build my fortune for over forty years now. It didn't come easy. And you know what else?" He stared at the young man intently. "You're absolutely right. It hasn't really done anyone any darned good, except my accountant. Until now." He took another puff. "So if my fellow Jews are suffering, it's about time I did something about it. Like you said, I'm not going to take it all with me, am I?"

He called over his son and issued clear directions.

"Write up whatever that young man over there tells you and sign my name to everything. Whatever money it takes to bring these Jews to America, make sure he gets it."

The son tried to dissuade him, but he was resolute.

"I want to have something to show for all my work, something more than just a load of figures on a balance sheet. I've got forty years of neglect to make up for, and there's no better time to do it than now."

A HOME FOR THE HOMELESS

In late 1938, Tress convened an emergency meeting of his Zeirei board. A crisis was confronting their operations. Desperate pleas for help were pouring in daily to Zeirei's Refugee and Immigration Division. There was absolutely insufficient space in the Zeirei's basement-level office to accommodate both the visitors and the paperwork their requests stimulated. A new, more spacious office was essential. Yet that would absorb much-needed funds from Zeirei's tiny coffers.

"Don't despair," Tress cautioned. "Hashem wants us to do our best. If we provide our top effort, I'm sure He'll provide the means. But understand me clearly. I'm not talking here of just another few feet of office space. I'm thinking of a place that will provide a whole battlefront of operations, all under one roof. That way, we can not only help bring refugees over but also take care of them when they arrive."

They found their answer in an imposing four-story brownstone building in Williamsburg at 616 Bedford Avenue, between Hooper and Hewes Streets. It had once served as a parish house for the church next door. The church had become the Hewes Street Shul, and the former parish house became "the location" for any European refugee seeking help. Its purchase by Zeirei was attained through the aid of generous benefactors, and by the spring of 1939, it was open for public use.

The gala *chanukas habayis* attracted a crowd too large to fit into the newly-acquired structure. Instead, the assemblage went to the nearby Clymer Street Shul to hear the stirring words of distinguished *rabbonim*. Yet, perhaps the most memorable address of all came from the former public school student and business administrator, Elimelech "Mike" Tress.

Speaking in his rousing style, brimming with confidence and *bitachon*, he swept the audience up in the soaring flight of his vision.

"They call America the *treifene medinah*," he said. "That may have been the case until now, but the tide is turning. Let us look forward to a different future, an America in which *yeshivos* will thrive and *Yiddishkeit* will blossom. Let us begin planning for a time when our children will aspire to be not primarily doctors or lawyers but *talmidei chachamim* and *baalei chessed*. And let us hope for a time when Jews of all different walks of life—*rabbonim, baalei battim, Chassidim* and *Misnagdim*—will work together to spread the eternal values of the Torah.

"War clouds loom over Europe. Our people face unimaginable hardships in the days ahead. But we cannot lose hope, no matter what happens. Our belief in Hashem must remain firm, and our reliance on His goodness must override all doubts. It is up to us, the members of His holy nation, to reclaim as much of our endangered heritage as we can, and to rebuild whatever has been destroyed."

These were fine words, but Tress's actions spoke even more loudly. The new Zeirei building was now a reality, and he and his *chaverim* found themselves dispensing public service beyond anything they had earlier imagined.

The building's four stories housed an array of activities. Its offices became magnets for those needing information and advice on the ever-changing government immigration regulations. The staff of the Refugee and Immigration Division, mainly young unmarried men, helped them fill out the increasingly complex forms needed to bring a loved one to safety. And now that more refugees were arriving, they were often at a loss for a dwelling. Any immigrant without a home was welcome to stay at 616. Some remained for weeks, others for months and even years. In all cases, they were treated not like anonymous boarders but like family.

Finally, 616 also served as the center for the Zeirei *minyan* and for the *Shabbos Pirchei* youth activities. In short, it was a bustling beehive of lifesaving activity, offering as many services as any government agency possibly could, but with a much friendlier face. After all, its administrators saw their efforts as not a contractual obligation but a holy privilege. They were helping their fellow Jews.

AN AMATEUR ARMY

For a small organization, Zeirei's goals were awesome. That young men were willing to take on the problems of a world gone wildly awry, and accomplish so much, was due to a remarkably selfless army of workers, led by a general who showed the way.

They worked together with members of the older generation, whose own achievements and examples proved how much could be done. They were inspired by Rabbi Eliezer Silver, the founder of Vaad Hatzalah, who had just to receive a request for aid to be off raising funds. They were bolstered by the success of Rabbi Dr. Leo Jung, who personally acquired over a thousand affidavits for refugees overseas. And they saw the generosity of men like Rav Eliezer Silver, Louis Septimus and others, who donated or raised vast amounts of money for the cause and often put their business affairs on hold to solicit funds for others.

Yet, in the end, it was the day-in, day-out labor of the Zeirei staff that made the difference. Many were volunteers, learning or working during the day and coming down to the office every night to address envelopes or make calls. Others worked full-time, ten to fifteen hours a day or more at the rate of ten to fifteen dollars a week. And in many cases, the workers used up even that meager amount to pay for postage stamps or overdue phone bills for the organization.

Such dedication pays eloquent tribute not only to their own efforts, but also to the man leading them. The workers invested so much energy in their work because they saw Mike Tress investing even more. They gave one hundred percent of themselves, because they watched Mike give one hundred and ten percent. They were all aware that he had given up a lucrative business career to toil ceaselessly for nearly nothing. They admired his friendly, informal manner and his hands-on style of solving problems. Every day, there were meetings, sometimes with high officials in Washington, sometimes with *"poshite Yiddin"* needing help with their legal forms. Mike treated them all the same and never said no to any request. Sometimes, his ingenious solutions to problems astonished even his co-workers.

"Please, Mr. Tress. I beg of you, do something!"

It was a common plea, but Tress didn't devote any less attention to it.

In this case, it was a woman telling of the plight of her husband. "He's in Finland, and he can't get out! He keeps trying to get approval to enter the United States, and he has all the papers. But he's missing a Swedish transit visa, and without it, they won't let him go."

"Have you written to the Swedish Consulate here about it?" Tress asked her.

"Yes. Once, twice, three times. But nothing helps. That's why I came to you. Someone said you are a miracle worker."

"If that were so, I would have ended this war years ago. No, let's leave the miracles to Hashem. But let's keep trying and praying. I'm sure He will make it all work out."

After she left, Tress conferred with his *chaverim*.

"Maybe we should try the Swedish Consulate again?" one of them suggested.

"No, we'll just get the same run-around," Tress replied. He rapped his fingers on the desk. "Maybe it's time for something a little more daring. What do you think?"

The others agreed.

One suggested the tactic eventually used. "Why don't we cable the King of Sweden directly?"

It was certainly daring, and very presumptuous. After all, who were they to communicate with a King? But then again, they reasoned, they were agents of the *Melech Malchei Hamelachim*, so why not try?

And so it was that His Royal Highness, King Gustav V of Sweden received an urgent communique from a group of young Jews in Brooklyn: "Help release our brother!"

A few days later, the phone rang. It was a caller from the Swedish Embassy. "His Royal Majesty has asked me to reply to your cable."

Tress was struck speechless with shock and amazement. He'd never thought he'd get any sort of answer. When he regained his composure, he said, "Thank you. Tell me, can anything be done to help this man?"

"He was allowed to leave this morning, on His Majesty's command. He should be arriving in the United States shortly."

Tress just barely managed to stifle his jubilation. "Thank you. Thank you ever so much."

"Well, His Majesty asks me to thank you for your admirable concern."

Not all cases were so dramatic, but many ended just as happily. In its 1941 report, Zeirei noted that during the first nine months of the year, it had procured nine hundred and forty affidavits for hopeful refugees–with each affidavit serving an entire family. Over four hundred of these families had since arrived in the United States. The numbers may seem paltry in view of the millions who eventually died. Still, for several thousand men, women and children, the affidavits secured by Zeirei during this time gave them a chance to start over in a free land.

For those who could not be brought over immediately, there were other offerings: funds and furnishings to keep them going; religious articles that helped them keep up their faith; words of encouragement that were truly priceless. If Tress and his *chaverim* could bolster the spirits of any Jew anywhere, they used every opportunity to do so.

As a result, Zeirei shipped *Sifrei Torah, mezuzos, siddurim* and *taleisim* to a variety of lands, such as Shanghai, Australia and Trinidad. When Jewish refugees escaped to the Philippines, there was no kosher food available for them. A member of the group eventually wrote to Zeirei for help.

Shortly afterwards, right before *Yom Kippur* of 1940, a letter arrived for the Jews in the Philippines. In it was the then-princely sum of five hundred dollars to pay for a Jew to go to Shanghai (where there was a sizable Jewish community headed by Rabbi Meir Ashkenazi) for training as a *shochet*.

"It was the most remarkable *Yom Kippur* experience we have had in some time," came back the response. "Our small group's dreams seem to have come true."

Those who made it to America received help that was even more all-encompassing. The rooms of 616 remained open to them as a refuge from poverty, indifference and loneliness. The shell-shocked escapees from the overseas inferno could find some peace of mind in this cost-free lodging, living among like-minded Jewish friends. Here, *frum* Jews could join in the *minyanim* and *Shabbos seudos* such as they had once known in Europe.

Above all, they could rest assured that Elimelech Tress would do everything humanly possible to help them. They knew he refused no one. He held no office hours. In fact, his services were never confined to an office setting. People approached him on his way to *Shacharis* or on his way home from *Maariv* at Yeshivah Torah Vodaath, then in Williamsburg. If they had a problem buying food or paying *yeshivah* tuition for their children, they could rely on him to deal with it. For those who needed medical treatment, he secured the services of a Dr. Friedman, a *Shomer Shabbos* Jew who set aside Wednesdays to give free assistance to patients who couldn't pay. And if they were ready to go out on their own and gain employment, he was always available if they needed further support.

Did someone require job training or placement? Tress had business connections who could provide it. Did someone need a truck to make his new store operational? Suddenly, it was there, courtesy of Tress. After all, helping someone stand on his own feet is the highest form of *tzedakah*.

Among those who made 616 their home was Josef Rosenberger, who'd fled from Germany after being held prisoner in the Dachau camp. At first, he was alone and lost, but he found a new meaning to life through the concern of the members of Zeirei. Tress encouraged him to use his scientific expertise for the benefit of the *klal*. He encouraged Rosenberger in his search for a solution to the problem of *shatnes*. For five years, he lived at 616 Bedford Avenue, where he set up his first *shatnes* laboratory, and eventually, he came up with a clever, inexpensive way of testing for *shatnes* in garments. This lay the foundation for the famed Shatnes Laboratory that still serves Jews today. One *mitzvah* had given birth to another, in a most fitting way.

SAVING THE *KLEI KODESH*

Like other Orthodox rescue activists, the Zeirei workers offered aid to anyone in need–religious or irreligious, *Chassid* or *Misnaged*, young or old. However, what really fired up their energy was the prospect of saving the scholars of the Holy Torah. They were aware that the true source of *Klal Yisrael's* well-being lay in the survival of these preservers of tradition.

Because the vast majority of the world's Orthodox Jews resided in Europe before the war, thousands of outstanding *talmidei chachamim* were among Hitler's intended victims. These included outstanding *gedolim*, as well as their *talmidim*, blossoming scholars about to be snuffed out. Eminent *yeshivos* with their flourishing student bodies were in mortal danger. They had to be preserved; they had to be brought to safety. This was Zeirei's top priority.

They strove valiantly to achieve it, using every means at their disposal. But they ran into a stubborn obstacle—the anti-immigration mood of the American public.

Ever since the 1920s, the United States government had been tightening its restrictions on immigration. This policy, boosted by wide popular support, was reinforced by the woes of the Great Depression. The average American had a hard enough time gaining employment before the war. Who needed a foreigner coming over and stealing jobs?

These feelings intensified with the outbreak of war, especially when even mighty nations like France fell to the Nazis. How had the Germans gotten so powerful? Americans were certain Nazi spies were operating within the United States (and in fact, several were). From then on, every European refugee was viewed with suspicion. Maybe he really was a foreign agent in disguise? This hysteria reached its height when California shipped thousands of Japanese-American residents off to detention camps to ensure that they weren't aiding the enemy. This paralleled similar sentiments in Canada and England, where Jewish immigrants were interned on the Isle of Man. Needless to say, this did not help the cause of those innocent victims seeking refuge.

"But why would a Jew spy for Hitler?" asked Jewish organizations. "Would he help someone pledged to destroy him?"

This logic fell on deaf ears. The restrictions on immigration were tightened.

Then there was another reason for this anti-immigrant sentiment, though it often went unexpressed. It was rooted in the ugly word "prejudice." The Depression of the 1930s gave rise to rabble-rousers playing on the fears and frustrations of the public. There was a reason for the widespread suffering, said those like Father Charles Coughlin and Fritz Kuhn (head of the pro-Nazi Bund). It all stemmed from the evil designs of the devilish, greedy Jew, who was out to master the world. Such respected American heroes as Henry Ford and Charles Lindbergh publicly echoed these anti-Jewish feelings. "The Jew is too powerful; he is dangerous," they kept repeating.

"He must be kept out of America." President Franklin Roosevelt lacked the courage to challenge these views. The defenseless European Jew was the victim of this mad myth.

American Jewish groups tried in vain to have the stiff immigration laws loosened during this time of crisis. The government remained unmoved.

Finally, though, as Hitler's oppression grew more obviously brutal, a ray of hope appeared. The regular immigration would not be increased. However, certain intellectuals and scholars judged to be imperiled would be admitted to the United States through Emergency Visas. The Jewish Labor Committee came up with a list of endangered intellectuals. Following suit, other groups, including the Orthodox, submitted their own lists to the government. There was hope at last, and the Zeirei workers toiled feverishly to win freedom for those on the Orthodox list.

But still another problem arose, and this time it wasn't the government. Instead, the threat came from none other than their fellow American Jews. They looked askance at the efforts to save *yeshivah* students, saying, "Who needs these strange-looking, foreign-sounding supporters of old-hat tradition? Why should we modern Jews be associated with them in the eyes of the public? Who needs them to slow our integration into American society?"

The Orthodox leadership labored hard to overcome this attitude. But even such dynamic individuals as Rabbi Avraham Kalmanowitz and Rabbi Eliezer Silver couldn't counter these sentiments. Certainly, Elimelech Tress and his co-workers did their best to reverse the trend. Tress flew out to Washington weekly to try to persuade the government to ease its stand. Twice, he was able to increase the number of Orthodox Jews eligible for Emergency Visas. But in the end, only about forty such individuals were able to benefit from these special papers. Among them were Rabbi Aharon Kotler, the future *rosh yeshivah* of Beth Medrash Govoha in Lakewood; Rabbi

Reuven Grozovsky, future *rosh yeshivah* of Yeshivah Torah Vodaath and head of Agudath Israel's Moetzes Gedolei Hatorah; Rabbi Elya Meir Bloch, Rabbi Mottel Katz and Rabbi Baruch Sorotzkin, all of the Telshe Yeshivah; Rabbi Simcha Zissel Levovits of the Mirrer Yeshivah; Rabbi Moshe Shatzkes and his son Rabbi Aharon; Rabbi David Lifschitz; Rabbi Shaul Yedidya Taub, the Modzhitser Rebbe; and the widow, son, daughter and son-in-law of the revered Chafetz Chaim.

That was certainly not enough to help the *talmidim* of the Mirrer Yeshiva. All five hundred of them had managed a miraculous escape to Kobe, Japan, before the war. However, every desperate attempt by Zeirei to bring them over to the United States, including the use of Paraguayan passports, proved unsuccessful. In the end, the members of the *yeshivah* were forced to relocate to Shanghai, under the control of Hitler's ally, the Japanese.

If Tress and his co-workers could not bring the Mirrer *rebbeim* and *talmidim* to America, they could at least send life-sustaining aid to them overseas–and they did. While they were located in Kobe, Zeirei joined with Vaad Hatzalah in dispatching Rabbi Frank Newman, a *musmach* of Yeshivah Torah Vodaath, as a special emissary. During his stay, Rabbi Newman saw to the settleing of the *yeshivos* in the Japanese sector of Shanghai as well as the needs of the *yeshivos*, dispensing food and funds, as well as spiritual uplifting. Together with Rabbi Avraham Kalmanowitz, he arranged for the shipment of two hundred copies of *Mesechtas Kiddushin* to be sent to Japan for the use of the *bnei yeshivah*.

REB AHARON KOTLER

Of all the great *rabbonim* saved from the European inferno to illuminate a future generation, perhaps the most illustrious was Rabbi Aharon Kotler.

The *gadol,* who was to found the Lakewood Yeshivah
and invigorate Torah Orthodoxy with his dynamic leadership,
was acclaimed a youthful *iluy* (prodigy) in his hometown of
Slutsk, Poland. By the age of nine, he had mastered the entire
Mesechte Kiddushin. Later, he more than fulfilled his early
promise, serving as *rosh yeshivah* in Kletzk and gaining fame
not only as a legendary *lamdan* but also a devoted leader of
the *klal.*

As a Torah giant, he earned the enmity of the Russian
Communists, who added him to their list of subversives and
harassed him whenever they could. By late 1940, after being
taken in for questioning by Russian agents, he had come to the
conclusion that his Torah institution could not survive under
Communist domination. He therefore decided to come to
America and try to transfer his *yeshivah* (then relocated to
Lithuania) to the free world. Rav Schorr made sure to have the
rosh yeshivah's name included at the head of lists of those in
line for an Emergency Visitor's Visa to the United States. After
hard work, a visa had been prepared for him in Moscow. His
evacuation from Europe seemed assured.

Shabbos had come none too soon for an exhausted
Elimelech Tress. That week, he had to work even beyond his
usual wide capacities, handling one emergency call after
another. The frigid winter winds and the swirling snow made
him doubly glad to be resting contentedly indoors after the
Shabbos seudah.

The shrillness of a doorbell disrupted his peace. Looking
out, he saw a Western Union messenger, and he knew that
meant an emergency. The cable he read confirmed it: "Came
to American Embassy in Moscow to receive Emergency Visa.
Was told none was waiting. Staff knows nothing about it. Must
leave Moscow within twenty-four hours. Please assist." It was
signed, simply, "Aharon Kotler."

The great Reb Aharon in trouble! Tress's exhaustion
dissipated in a flash as plans and ideas flooded his brain. If any

problem needed immediate resolution, he knew, this was it. The Russians allowed no more than twenty-four hours for individuals to complete their immigration affairs before they were driven out of Moscow. This foul-up regarding visas had to be cleared up by then, and according to Tress's calculations, judging by the time on the telegram, Reb Aharon had only nine more hours to go. After that, he would be sent away, probably to oblivion.

As in all crises, Tress immediately conferred with others. Rushing over to his very close friend and trusted advisor Rav Gedaliah Schorr, he explained the situation. Together, they decided to consult Rabbi Shlomo Heiman, *rosh yeshivah* of Yeshivah Torah Vodaath, to confirm their opinion that the sanctity of *Shabbos* should not stand in the way of action in this case.

Rabbi Heiman did not hesitate. "If I had the power, I would personally type up the visa for Reb Aharon this very minute!"

The next stop was at the home of Moshe Berger, the head of Zeirei's Immigration Bureau and an expert at filling out the complicated visa forms. The three raced to 616 Bedford Avenue and, at 10:30 p.m., began filling out the necessary legal papers. First, though, they closed the window shutters tight, so as not to give those ignorant of the situation any impression of *chilul Shabbos*.

By four o'clock in the morning, they had finished the grueling task of writing up all the forms for a new visa. Sending the others back to their homes for some sleep, Tress insisted on carrying the task to its conclusion. Stopping briefly at home to freshen up, he was off to Washington to beat the deadline.

His train arrived in the capital city of Washington just before ten o'clock in the morning. Icy winds and treacherous streets greeted his arrival, but otherwise the nation's capital was hardly astir. Arriving at the State Department Building without the benefit of an appointment, Tress wandered the winding hallways. It was not, of course, a work day in the government building. Yet, perhaps someone was in and willing to help him out.

He knocked on door after door. No answer. No one was around.

Then, from a distance, he noticed a faint glimmer of light filtering through the bottom of a door. The sign said, "Office of the Assistant Secretary of State." Perhaps a secretary had come in; maybe she could locate someone for him.

He knocked and came face-to-face with the Undersecretary of State himself, Breckenridge Long.

Tress was stunned and also dismayed. Long was a major diplomat. He had dealings with him before and had often come away disappointed. Long was not at all known as a friend of Jewish refugees.

Long stared back at him in a puzzled way.

"You're Mr. Tress, aren't you?" he finally said. "I recognized you from a meeting a while back. What brings you to Washington?"

"It's a true emergency, sir."

"I realized that," Long replied. "Only an emergency would have brought you out here on your Sabbath. I know how holy you hold this day. Please have a seat and tell me how I can help you."

Tress explained the situation and stressed the urgency due to the time element involved. Long nodded, and without asking any further questions, he rose and took Tress to the State Department's secret "code room." There, they quickly cabled all the important information about Reb Aharon to the American Embassy in Moscow, hoping to beat the looming deadline.

"And make sure to bring this applicant to the embassy by staff car, so that he can get his visa immediately," Long told the employee at the other end of the line. "This man is a most prominent and important scholar, and he must be helped quickly."

Tress thanked Long effusively and then left. The wait for a reply began.

It arrived the next Tuesday, and it was not hopeful. The Embassy hadn't been able to find Rabbi Kotler, and he hadn't returned on his own. In all probability, Reb Aharon had gone somewhere else. Tress knew he had tried his best, but the deep and gnawing anxiety over Reb Aharon's fate depressed him greatly.

Two weeks later, the phone rang at 616. The operator announced that the call was from Kobe, Japan, and Tress knew that it was Rabbi Frank Newman, reporting on attempts to get visas for the *talmidim* there.

It was indeed Rabbi Newman, but he immediately said, "Someone else here would like to speak to you," and relinquished the receiver.

A second later, Tress heard an unfamiliar energetic voice pronounce in a rapid staccato, "This is Aharon Kotler."

The sage explained to a much-relieved Elimelech Tress what had happened. With the deadline for leaving Moscow approaching, Reb Aharon had placed his trust in Hashem and taken his chances. Despite the lack of a visa, he had gone to board the train that would take him across Siberia. At the station, he noticed to his dismay that a Russian official was looking straight at him. Would he be stopped so close to success? Not revealing any fear, Reb Aharon had stared back, and for some inexplicable reason, the official turned away.

After the arduous six-thousand-mile journey across the vast expanses of Russia, Reb Aharon arrived in Vladivostok, only to confront another Communist official checking passengers' papers. Once again, Reb Aharon showed no sense of fright. And once again, he was allowed to move on. Hashem had spared the sage's life.

In Japan, Reb Aharon received word that the American

Embassy in Moscow had, thanks to the persistent efforts of the Zeirim, issued him a visa. He arrived in San Francisco on *Erev Pesach*, 1941, and during *Chol Hamoed* took the train to New York.

There, he was greeted by a joyous throng of *rabbonim*, as well as hundreds of Zeirei and Pirchei youths. Many had been assembled for the occasion by Elimelech Tress, and in welcoming Reb Aharon, these young Americans gained a new realization. Not sports figures or entertainment leaders but *Gedolei Torah* were authentic heroes to be acclaimed and treasured by Jews of all ages.

Reb Aharon wasn't interested in receiving great honors. When speaking to the welcoming crowd, he ignored his own experiences and concentrated on those left behind. "On the other side of the ocean, our brothers are waiting for our help. Only you, the Jews of America, can aid them. Do it now! Save them!"

Given a forum by Zeirei Agudath Israel, Reb Aharon immediately plunged into rescue work. He helped direct the activities of Vaad Hatzalah, together with Rabbi Avraham Kalmanowitz and Rabbi Eliezer Silver, and spurred his colleagues to ever bolder rescue plans.

Accompanied by Elimelech Tress, he made frequent and numerous trips to Washington, speaking to any public official who might be of assistance. When Secretary of Treasury Henry Morgenthau protested that speaking out on behalf of Jews might cost him his job, Reb Aharon replied, "One Jewish life is worth more than thousands of positions like yours."

Reb Aharon avoided petty politics and downplayed differences among Jews in this urgent work. And when some criticized him for working with non-religious Jews in this area, he didn't flinch. "I would bow before the Pope if that would help save the fingernail of even one Jewish child," he declared.

After the war, Reb Aharon further expanded his activist

work on behalf of Torah institutions. As chairman of Agudah's Moetzes Gedolei Hatorah and director of Chinuch Atzmai and numerous other organizations, he proved that Torah could indeed thrive in America.

His survival enabled him to usher in a whole new era in the history of American Orthodox Judaism. Torah, though battered and sent scurrying, was no longer an imperiled orphan.

SELFLESS TO THE END

Like Reb Aharon Kotler, Elimelech Tress was eager to co-operate with anyone willing to join in the task of *hatzalah*. As Zeirei's operations expanded, it received the active assistance of such diverse rabbinical figures as the Boyaner Rebbi, the Novominsker Rebbi and Kapichenitzer Rebbe, Rabbi Dr. Joseph Breuer of Washington Heights, Rabbi Pinchas Teitz of Elizabeth, New Jersey, Rabbi Joseph Soloveitchik of Boston and the remarkable founder of Torah Umesorah and other educational institutes Rabbi Shraga Feivel Mendlowitz.

In addition, the group benefitted from the incisive advice and financial support of such business leaders and community activists as Irving Bunim, Henry Hirsch, Joseph Rosenzweig, Hirsch Manischewitz and many others. They also worked hand in hand with other rescue organizations such as Vaad Hatzalah and the Sternbuchs' HIJEFS. As far as Tress was concerned, all offers of help were accepted, even from the least experienced benefactors.

During the war itself, Tress played a crucial role in numerous rescue projects, such as the Kastner Train and the Musy mission. His efforts led him to make numerous trips to Washington, often at a moment's notice, to gain government support for these initiatives. And he helped coordinate programs closer to home, too.

The members of the Zeirei *minyan* at 616 were about to hear the *leining* of the *Haftorah* one *Shabbos* morning in 1944, when a cable arrived from Rabbi Michoel Ber Weissmandl. Funds were needed desperately to help save Hungarian Jewry. If immediate aid were not forthcoming, the last chance to rescue them might be lost.

Word of this reached Reb Gedaliah Schorr, one of Tress's most cherished *chaverim*. Visibly shaken, he went silently to the *bimah*. The *mispallelim* waited for a brief announcement. Instead, they were stunned to see Reb Gedalya smash his fist down on the podium with all his might. Now brimming with concern, they noticed large tears streaming down his face.

"*Rabbosai*, how dare we think of our personal interests at a time like this? How can we be concerned with our jobs, our welfare, even our advancement in learning? *Gevalt!* Jewish lives can be saved for the price of a few dollars, and we just sit around doing nothing? Where is our conscience? Don't we realize that any moment might be too late?"

The *divrei mussar* hit home. There could be no containing the will of the Zeirim to act. At the behest of Tress and Rabbi Schorr, principals closed down their *yeshivos* to allow *talmidim* to help carry out the drive for funds. Some sat by the phones for three days straight to solicit aid. Others joined groups that went out to collect money in the streets, in the subways, at meetings of Jewish organizations and from door to door. As young as they were, they, too, had a part in this overwhelming *mitzvah* of saving Jewish lives. In the end, some one hundred thousand dollars–an enormous sum in those days, especially for such a small organization–was raised.

It was just in this light, as a *mitzvah* commanded by the Torah, that Elimelech Tress viewed his *hatzalah* activities. He saw his work not as a nine-to-five job but as a special privilege granted him by Hashem, a chance to be *podeh shvuyim* who would otherwise be lost to the *klal*. So he took his work home with him every day, inviting new immigrants to his *Shabbos* meals, often a dozen at a time, and accepting requests for help at any time of the day, precisely because it wasn't work. It was his life.

Even when the war ended, therefore, the work wasn't over. There were no additional Jews to save from the Nazis, but there were thousands of Jews wasting away in Displaced Persons Camps in Europe. Zeirei shipped as many packages crammed with essential goods to them as it could. Then Tress decided on a risky gambit. He would make the dangerous trip to Europe to visit the camps himself, one of the first American Jews to do so. That way, the *chizuk* could be applied directly, as the survivors would see in person that their fellow Jews were eager to help them.

What he saw there, the broken remains of what had once been princely, robust dynamos of *Yiddishkeit*, appalled him. He set out at once, offering comfort and all the material goods he could provide, especially his own. He came laden with possessions and left emptyhanded, without even the socks on his feet.

Those in the Displaced Persons Camps were most grateful for his selfless contributions, but the trip took a grueling toll on him. Friends who welcomed him after his return said that he had aged considerably. After seeing just how devastating the war had been for Europe's Jews, he was never again the same jovial Mike they had known.

Nevertheless, his efforts on behalf of the *klal* continued and even intensified. He moved up to the helm of the Zeirei's parent organization, Agudath Israel of America, and helped spur it to become one of the country's foremost Orthodox organizations, guided by the *Daas Torah* of its rabbinical advisors. He was also active in rebuilding on American soil the *yeshivos* that had perished during the war, such as the Telshe Yeshiva.

His overworked body gave out in 1967, when he was only fifty-eight. He did not leave behind a wealth of money; he had given up his business career to work for Zeirei, and he had sold valuable stocks to help finance the founding of Camp Agudah. However, the wealth of his life's accomplishments was incalculable. He had helped save thousands of lives, had enriched many thousands more and had played a major role in making Orthodoxy a strong and viable force on the American scene.

Not everyone aided by Zeirei expressed their gratitude, and Tress was not one who sought glory. But many righteous men and women realized just how indebted they were to Elimelech Tress for their very survival.

The meeting of Agudah executive officers was running late, and the last item on the agenda was being discussed. Suddenly, there was a knock at the door. A man entered, his beard and stately bearing identifying him as a Torah scholar. The others rose to greet him.

"Excuse me," he said softly. "I am sorry to interrupt. I am late coming here because I am new to America. I have just come from Shanghai, with my *chaverim* from the Mirrer Yeshivah. I will not keep you long. Please tell me, which of you gentlemen is Elimelech Tress?"

The others pointed out their smiling colleague in the middle.

Without a word, the scholar walked over to Tress and, with tears glistening in his eyes, embraced him. Then he embraced the others too, each in turn. Finally, he stood back to make a little speech.

"*Rabbosai*, you do not know, you cannot realize, what you mean to all of us from the *yeshivah*. When we were on the run from one refuge to another, never knowing what tomorrow would bring, two things kept us going. One, of course, was our steadfast *emunah* in Hashem. The other was the knowledge that you here at Zeirei would do everything you could to help us.

"Words of thanks do not even begin to repay you. Let me just say that if anyone truly understands the meaning of the statement, *Kol Yisrael areivim zeh lazeh*, it is you. May Hashem bless you all. And may He save a special *berachah* for your chairman, and our most beloved friend, the remarkable *klal* worker Reb Elimelech Gavriel Tress."

The World Must Be Told

MR. GEORGE MANTELLO

George (Mandel) Mantello, the Jewish First Secretary of El Salvador in Switzerland, protected the lives of thousands of Jews by sending them El Salvador citizenship papers free of cost. Through an intensive publicity effort, he also accomplished the extraordinary feat of halting deportations from Budapest to Auschwitz, saving tens of thousands of Jewish lives.

4 — THE WORLD MUST BE TOLD

MR. GEORGE MANTELLO

ON APRIL 7, 1944, THE SIRENS AT AUSCHWITZ SHRIEKED AN alarm: *"Jewish inmates have escaped!"*

The Nazi camp commandants were dumfounded. Breaking out of Auschwitz was considered virtually impossible. The camp was surrounded by extremely tall fences lined with high-tension barbed wire, guaranteeing that anyone who touched them was instantly electrocuted. Behind the walls were deep ditches. Watchtowers manned by Nazi guards with machine guns were positioned throughout the camp. Those who somehow managed to evade these traps were tracked down by the vicious guard dogs favored by the S.S. By these sinister precautions, the Nazis hoped to ensure that no camp prisoner would ever be able to flee and thereby alert outsiders to the nightmarish world of Auschwitz.

Yet two Jews managed to outwit them.

Alfred Wetzler and Walter Rosenberg (later known as Josef Lanik and Rudolf Vrba) knew the odds against a successful getaway. Still, they felt compelled to make the attempt.

155

The Nazis had put them to work as clerks in the camp, and in this capacity they had access to a vast amount of information. All the data and sights they'd seen confirmed the bitter truth: Any Jew brought to Auschwitz-Birkenau (as the combined camps were known) was doomed to almost certain death. It might be immediate; it might be delayed. But whether through gassings or beatings or back-breaking work, the inmates were being systematically destroyed. Not dozens, not hundreds, but thousands. Daily. All before their very eyes.

Why wasn't the outside world doing anything to thwart the Nazis? Could it be that they weren't aware of what was going on? If so, who would tell them?

They were therefore determined to break out of the camp. Not only to save themselves but to save their fellow inmates. They would have to inform an ignorant world of the incredible truth.

With the help of other camp inmates, they managed to build a hiding place sunk deep into the ground, hidden by boards and other bits of wood. When it was ready, they waited for an opportune time. Then, at night, they broke from their barracks and concealed themselves inside. And waited.

The absence was quickly noticed. As the inmates were subjected to inhumanly lengthy roll calls, and as the guards searched the barracks, the chief officers nodded confidently among themselves. The escapees would soon be back, dead or alive. The guard dogs would see to that.

But Wetzler and Rosenberg had thought of dealing with the dogs, too. They had put gasoline-soaked tobacco all around their hiding place, and this had the desired effect. It completely threw off the dogs' sense of smell, and they failed to detect the two fugitives. When the dogs returned to their masters without any clues, the Nazis were shocked and furious. But the Jews permitted themselves brief smiles of satisfaction.

The two men remained in their shelter for three long

days. By then, cooped up in the stifling hole with a rapidly diminishing supply of food and water, they had almost gone mad. They were close to abandoning their scheme when they heard someone order the nearby guard to leave his post. That was their signal to act. Under cover of darkness, they crawled behind the empty watchtower, under the front gate and out to freedom.

After a hazardous ten-day flight, they managed to cross the border into Slovakia. Soon they had established contact with the Jewish underground—the so-called Working Group—which was operating there. The members of the group, led by Rabbi Michoel Ber Weissmandl, listened in numbed outrage as the two men reported in gruesome detail their stupefying experiences and observations at Auschwitz.

When they finished their account, there was a horrified silence. Finally, one of the group whispered, "This is worse than we ever possibly imagined." No more rumors, no more speculation. They knew the truth now, as depicted by eyewitnesses. The horrors could no longer be denied.

Compounding the sense of anguish was the escapees' report that the mass murders were about to be stepped up. The Nazis had just begun enlarging Auschwitz. They were making room for the Jews of Hungary, which the German armies had just conquered. In fact, starting in May 1944, the Nazis did indeed begin speeding Hungarian Jews off to Auschwitz at a rate of twelve thousand a day.

The members of the Working Group knew that this first-hand account of the horrors of Auschwitz had to reach the free world. Perhaps it would finally arouse the conscience of humankind and prompt some action before Hungarian Jewry was totally destroyed.

Therefore, they wrote up what Wetzler and Rosenberg had told the Working Group. This thirty-page report came to be called the Auschwitz Protocols. Rabbi Weissmandl compiled his own shorter Hebrew version and concluded it with an appeal to the Allies to bomb the railways to Auschwitz.

The Working Group then sent the report by paid messengers to Jewish leaders and organizations in Hungary and Switzerland. From there, it was transmitted to prominent groups and individuals in the free world, including diplomats and world leaders. Over and over, the point was emphasized: Here, at last, was a true, certifiable account of what the Nazis were really doing to Europe's Jews, told by men who had seen it happening. No one could any longer say that these were just exaggerations.

The heads of the underground waited for an angry, explosive reaction to the Protocols. But once again, the only response was silence.

Diplomats ignored the pleas, and newspapers eyed the story with skepticism. The Allied governments claimed they were too busy fighting the war to react, and even some Jewish groups were wary of presenting news of Jewish suffering too prominently. They were afraid this might undermine the war effort and turn it into a "Jewish issue." And then there were the usual scoffers who claimed the depictions of Nazi terror were all a pumped-up hoax.

Meanwhile, with each passing day, still more masses of Jews were sealed inside cramped cattle cars and sent on their way to Auschwitz's ovens.

Were the Nazis truly unstoppable? Could no one do anything to halt the slaughter of Hungarian Jews? Or would an unheeding world let Hitler and his henchmen press their "Final Solution" to its deadly conclusion?

And yet, only two months later, world leaders were up in arms. The American President, the heads of other countries and even the Pope were publicly condemning the deportation of Hungarian Jews to Auschwitz.

Newspapers started running banner headlines about the situation, and editorials in once-silent journals began blasting the Nazis for their despicable atrocities.

Stunned by this barrage of criticism, the nominal head of Hungary, Admiral Miklos Horthy, was emboldened to defy the Nazis. In early July, 1944, he ordered that the transport of Jews to Auschwitz be stopped immediately.

What had happened? What had prompted this sudden, dramatic turnaround?

To a large extent, it was due to a campaign launched by a single determined Jew. His name was George Mandel Mantello, and it can be argued that, by helping to stop the mass transport to Auschwitz of the one hundred and fifty thousand Hungarian Jews remaining in Budapest, he performed the greatest single act of Jewish rescue during the entire war.

FROM BUSINESSMAN TO DIPLOMAT

George Mandel Mantello was born in 1900 to an Orthodox Jewish family in Rumania that was prominently involved in religious causes. His grandfather Rabbi Yitzchak Yaakov Mandel had been a *rav* and *halachic* authority in Hungary, and George's father Yosef Yehuda Baruch Mandel had been a Talmudic student in his youth. George himself did not pursue the rabbinate, embarking instead on a business career. With his brother Joseph, he established a textile manufacturing plant, in partnership with several high-ranking Rumanian army officers. However, he always remained a faithful Jew, committed to the traditional Jewish ideal of assisting his fellow man whenever possible.

As a businessman, he had the opportunity to travel throughout Europe. Thus, he was in an uncommon position to view firsthand the Nazi terror campaign against Jews. In 1938, he was in Vienna, Austria, when German troops goosestepped across the border and seized control of the country. George Mantello witnessed Nazi storm troopers round up Jews all across the country. Thousands were thrown into jail, their property confiscated. For their amusement, German soldiers made pious Jews wipe the Nazi barracks clean with the straps of their holy *tefillin*.

Some time later, he was again on hand as the Germans took over Czechoslovakia in 1939, and once again in 1941, when they gained control over Yugoslavia. Throughout, he witnessed the Nazis' immediate steps to terrorize the Jewish population.

To Mantello, then, the persecution of Jews was not a hazy rumor but an observed fact. And the fact infuriated him. He felt an urgent need to act, to assist his fellow Jews. And as it turned out, he was in an uncommon position to do so.

Mantello's business dealings eventually brought him into contact with the political leaders of the small Central American country of El Salvador. The Salvadorans were impressed with his work and his generosity, and after he became a Salvadoran citizen in 1939, he was granted the title of honorary counsul for El Salvador, serving Czechoslovakia, Hungary and Yugoslavia. As an amateur diplomat, he now had many influential contacts.

That did not automatically guarantee his personal safety, though. He was in Belgrade, Yugoslavia, in 1942 when the pro-German regime ordered him held under surveillance. They suspected him (rightly so) of helping smuggle Jews out to Hungary and Rumania, and from there to the free world. Mantello was kept under house arrest in the hotel which served as his residence, and he remained there for several months. It was a very depressing period in his life, and he kept searching for a way out of his predicament.

Finally, he received a visit from a friend of General Draganescu, a World War I aviation hero, who was Mantello's former business partner in Rumania. The man had been sent by Draganescu expressly to save Mantello. He was a pilot, and he arrived at the hotel dressed in an aviator's uniform.

After locating Mantello, the man explained his mission,

"I've come to get you out of here."

"You don't know how much I appreciate your efforts," Mantello responded. "But it's no use. The authorities are keeping close tabs on me. They'll never let me leave."

The man removed his uniform, to reveal another uniform right under it.

"Here, put this on," he said.

Mantello did so.

"Good," said the pilot. "You look very dashing. From now on, you are with me. If anyone asks, you are my co-pilot."

With his new guise and changed identity, Mantello managed to sneak out of the hotel, along with the pilot. The latter brought him to his personal plane, and they took off, with Mantello as the "co-pilot." Soon they had put Yugoslavia behind them.

Because Rumania, too, had installed a pro-Nazi government, Draganescu flew the plane to Italy. From there, Mantello took a train to Switzerland, where his brother had settled a year earlier. Mantello now became the First Secretary of El Salvador's embassy in Geneva, Switzerland, a position that was to serve him well in his future rescue activities.

DIPLOMACY AT WORK

He edged into those activities slowly, drawn step by step into the battle for lives.

Others in his position would not even have bothered. Who needed the aggravation? After all, Mantello was well-respected and well-to-do. He could have settled for the easy life in serene Switzerland, pursuing his own private interests first and ignoring the calamities across the border. That, however, was not his way.

Instead, he began to seek the rescue of first one refugee, and then another. He had the advantage of his diplomatic status, which gave him access to numerous international officials. Making use of this, he was able to gain permission for several Jews to emigrate to safety.

The more he dabbled in rescue work, however, the more he saw the need for a full-scale rescue program. As a single individual, there was a limit to what he could accomplish. But if Jews as a group helped each other—if Jewish organizations joined to aid the European refugees—their efforts would be all the more effective.

It was an obvious idea. Too obvious, perhaps, because no one had ever really tried it before. It was clearly time to do so.

Mantello contacted the Jewish aid organizations with offices in Switzerland and invited their representatives to a meeting. He explained to them that if they pooled their considerable resources, they could accomplish an enormous amount. And the Jews of Europe needed every bit of help they could get.

Yes, of course, the organizations understood. They were in complete agreement. And they would be pleased to meet as part of a united front. That is, only if certain conditions were met.

For instance, they would have to approve the agenda. And they would come only if certain other organizations were not invited. It seems there were personality conflicts among some of the members. And then there were political disputes with others, and religious differences with yet others, so there could be no seeing eye-to-eye with them. And furthermore . .

Mantello sighed. He tried to bridge the gaps, but diplomacy could get him just so far. Despite the extreme urgency of the situation, he couldn't get the groups to overlook their differences and cooperate. They insisted on playing politics even as their brothers and sisters were dying.

Finally, Mantello decided to proceed on his own, together with whatever groups were willing to work with him

PRICELESS PAPERS

One of those who did cooperate was Maitre Matthieu Muller, who had long been one of the heads of the French branch of Agudath Israel. Muller and his family had managed to escape to Switzerland from Vichy France (the southern half of the nation, which had installed a government willing to collaborate with the Nazis). In Switzerland, he assisted the rescue activist Yisrael Chaim Eis in his work and gained invaluable expertise in preparing complicated documents needed for emigration. Eis introduced Muller to Mantello, and the two men pooled their resources. One of their most successful ventures expanded on a plan already in existence.

In 1941, the Sternbuchs had discovered that Jews who held foreign diplomatic papers were accorded privileged treatment by the Nazis. Thereupon, both they and Yisrael Chaim Eis had tried to provide as many Jews as possible with these precious documents. And indeed, the Nazis were careful not to abuse the possessors of these papers. Rather than deporting them to Auschwitz or Sobibor, they sent them instead to relatively placid camps like Vittel. The Germans kept them alive, hoping that, in exchange, German citizens in South America and elsewhere would be protected from harm.

Getting hold of these documents was hardly simple, though. Foreign diplomats were willing to provide these passports, but for a huge fee, usually charging anywhere from four hundred to three thousand Swiss francs each. Since neither Eis nor the Sternbuchs had access to enormous sums of money, this severely limited the number of passports they could obtain.

Now Mantello's diplomatic status became all-important.

Taking full advantage of his position, he rented an office in the name of the Salvadoran consulate. Under the direction of Maitre Muller, this was turned into a virtual factory for the issuance of Salvadoran citizenship papers. Getting these papers in order was no simple matter. They had to be painstakingly filled out, translated and copied. To help with this complex project, they recruited both Jewish and non-Jewish student volunteers who were able to spell the complicated Hungarian names and places that had to appear on the papers.

Mantello's team worked diligently and carefully to turn out document after document. The costs involved in preparing the documents were considerable, and Mantello covered them out from his own pocket. Then he went about distributing the papers to needy Jews—free of charge.

Other diplomats were furious at him. Here they were making a tidy profit selling South American papers and getting rich on the misery of others. Then Mantello came along and gave away the very same papers for nothing, thereby flooding the market and lowering the overall price. It simply wasn't fair!

Mantello ignored their protests and maintained his momentum. His object was to save lives, not to make a fortune. As John Winant, the American Ambassador to England, later wrote, Mantello "was the only one who acted from purely humanitarian motives" in issuing the papers. In the end, thousands of Salvadoran papers were printed and given out to Jews. And the sum total of those who benefitted was even greater, since many additional Jews forged their own copies based on Mantello's originals.

CRISIS!

At first, the Salvadoran papers provided remarkably effective protection, but in the spring of 1944, there was upsetting news. Word spread that the Nazis were reconsidering their hands-off attitude toward the possessors of the Latin American papers. They were beginning to doubt that the documents were valid and that their bearers deserved special protection.

Through his contacts, Mantello learned that the Germans had started asking various Latin American countries if they were willing to authenticate the papers and acknowledge responsibility for the Jews who held them.

This was the critical moment. If El Salvador repudiated Mantello's work, then all his efforts had been wasted. More significantly, it would mean that all those who had gotten the Salvadoran papers would suddenly become very vulnerable.

The wait was nerve-wracking. Finally, the situation became clear.

The Nazis were indeed challenging the Latin American papers, and most of the countries in whose names they had been issued were slow in validating them. Only after a desperate and lengthy campaign by Vaad Hatzalah, Agudath Israel, the Sternbuchs and others did many of the countries once again back up the papers. But by then, many of those who'd relied on the papers were dead.

Mantello was worried. Would the Salvadoran citizenship papers he had issued prove effective or would they turn out to be worthless? He awaited word from El Salvador.

At last it came. Upon the advice of his ambassadors, General Castenendu Castro, the Salvadoran President, announced that the documents had his full blessing. Whatever his Swiss representative had done was validated.

Those with Salvadoran papers were still safe. Ironically, some Jews had hesitated accepting Mantello's documents. They'd believed they were worthless because they were handed out for free and because they were citizenship papers rather than passports. Instead, these Jews had opted for the expensive papers issued by other lands, only to learn in the end that the costly documents were the less effective ones.

The results of Mantello's efforts continued to reverberate, to the benefit of the Jews. When Hungarian Jews were being rounded up in 1944, the papers he had issued–or forged copies of them–saved many a person. The legendary Raoul

Wallenberg and others were able to offer official protection to those who held them, and in this way, thousands avoided the murderous grasp of the Nazis.

A CHANCE DISCOVERY

By March 1944, had he so desired, Mantello could have relaxed and settled cozily into the comforts of Swiss life, confident that his reputation as a rescue activist was already secure. But that wasn't his way. There were still major tasks to tackle, still Jews in tremendous trouble.

As it turned out, his most formidable rescue achievements were yet to come. They were focused on the Jews of Hungary, the last sizable Jewish community left in East Europe. Eight hundred thousand strong, they had lived relatively peaceful lives during the war years under the generally benign rule of Hungary's leader Admiral Horthy. However, when word reached Hitler in early 1944 that Horthy was negotiating with the Allies, he ordered his troops into the country. Directed by Adolf Eichmann, the task of rounding up and deporting Hungary's Jews to the death camps began almost immediately. Among these Jews were Mantello's parents, whose hometown had been incorporated as part of Hungary.

With Hungary in German hands, communications between it and the outside world were cut off. Relatives of the trapped Jews, including George Mantello, were frantic for word of the welfare of their families. Mantello decided to take quick action.

He contacted a friend, Dr. E. Florian Manoliu, the Rumanian commercial attache in Bern, Switzerland, and asked him to undertake a dangerous mission to Hungary. The object of his trip was two-fold. First, he would investigate and report on what was happening to Hungarian Jewry. There had been a total news blackout in Hungary, imposed by the Nazis. Rumors of disaster for the Jews abounded, but more authentic information was needed. Second, he would hand out to Hungarian Jews a thousand Salvadoran papers that Mantello had already signed and certified.

Because Dr. Manoliu was both non-Jewish and a diplomat from Rumania, a Nazi ally, Mantello felt he stood a good chance of being allowed to travel through Europe without difficulty. Unfortunately, that wasn't the case. Manoliu set out for Hungary on May 22, 1944. As soon as he arrived in Vienna, he was arrested. The Germans knew he held anti-Nazi views, and that was cause enough to detain him. After a week of intensive questioning, Manoliu was released. Shaken but still resolute, he continued on his journey.

Manoliu's first stop was in the town of Bistritz, where Mantello's parents lived. He tracked down the address Mantello had given him and knocked at the door. The man who opened it, a burly peasant, was clearly not the person Manoliu had hoped to greet. But maybe this was only a boarder. Hopeful, he asked if there was anyone inside named Mandel (Mantello's original family name).

The man shrugged in response.

Manoliu tried again. "Can you tell me where the owner of the house is?"

"Owner? Me!" The man pointed emphatically at himself.

"Do you know where the head of the Jewish community is?"

"Jews?" The man guffawed loudly. "No Jews here, not anymore. All of them are far away. Far away."

The man waved his hand vaguely towards the north and grinned. Manoliu grinned back. He couldn't reveal his sympathy for the Jews without arousing suspicion.

Not giving up yet, Manoliu traveled from one town in Hungary to another, making cautious inquiries. Wherever he went, though, he found no trace of Jews. Clearly, he had arrived too late.

He knew Mantello would be devastated by the news.

Still, his journey had to continue. Perhaps there was yet time to save others.

On June 19, he arrived in Budapest and immediately arranged to see Charles Lutz, the Swiss consul. After Manoliu told him why he had come, Lutz considered for a moment.

"Come," he said. "There is someone I am sure you'll want to meet."

Lutz took him to the basement, where a man was sitting at a desk piled high with papers. Lutz introduced him as Moshe Krausz, the head of the Palestine Office, an agency involved with issuing immigration certificates for Palestine, as Israel was then called.

"Mr. Krausz is staying at the consulate for the time being, under my protection," Lutz explained. "It isn't safe for a Jew to be out on the street in Hungary anymore."

As Manoliu gave his own name and position, he noticed Krausz eyeing him carefully.

"You're not Jewish, are you?" Krausz asked.

"No, but I've come at the urging of George Mantello, the Salvadoran representative in Switzerland."

"I'm sorry, but I don't know him." Krausz was obviously, and understandably, suspicious.

Then Manoliu remembered something. He removed a card from his wallet and presented it to Krausz. The name on the card was Chaim Posner. There was Hebrew writing on it.

"Mr. Mantello suggested I present this note of reference by way of introduction," he said.

Krausz suddenly nodded in recognition.

"Of course," he said. "Chaim Posner is my counterpart in Switzerland. We're good friends."

Posner had written in Hebrew that both Mantello and Manoliu could be fully trusted, and this eased Krausz's mind considerably. Now their fateful discussions could begin.

Krausz gave Manoliu a relentlessly grim picture of the Hungarian situation. Since the Nazi takeover in March, the anti-Jewish measures had been enforced with astonishing speed. By now masters at murder, the Nazis had started deporting Jews in April, and through mid-June some three hundred and thirty thousand Jews had already been sent to Auschwitz. And the deportations were continuing at the rate of twelve thousand Jews each day.

Manoliu hardly knew what to say. On the verge of tears, he took out the documents Mantello had entrusted to him and handed them over to Krausz.

"There are a thousand Salvadoran citizenship papers here, all signed and ready to be used," said Manoliu. "All that has to be done is fill in the names of the families using them. A thousand may not be much, considering what's happening. But every life counts, I suppose."

Krausz received them warmly. Then, as an afterthought, he remarked, "Maybe I can send Mr. Mantello something in exchange. I have here a report that recently reached me from Slovakia. It's a first-hand account of what is actually happening at Auschwitz. I could hardly bear to read it. Then there's an additional report, about what has happened here since the Nazi occupation of Hungary. Please make sure Mr. Mantello goes through them carefully. Maybe he can somehow use them."

"I certainly will."

"And if it is not too much trouble, could you please take back a short letter to my friend Chaim Posner?"

Manoliu watched as Krausz poured his heart into an agonized written plea: "We have only a few days left. If the Christian world wants to do something to help us, then several thousand people can still be saved. But if not, may Heaven have mercy on us!"

When he was finished, Krausz handed over the letter, and shook Manoliu's hand with deep emotion.

"This may be the last time I see someone from the free world," he said.

"I'll convey your words to Mr. Posner and to anyone else I can. I was supposed to go on to Bucharest, but that can wait. It's far more important that I rush back to Switzerland with your messages. Don't worry. You won't be forgotten. Somehow, something *will* be done."

THE REPORTS HEARD AROUND THE WORLD

George Mantello's grief was almost beyond endurance. Upon his return, Dr. Manoliu had stunned him with two tragic pieces of news: the report of the calamitous mass murders at Auschwitz and the sad fact of his parents' probable deaths. It was enough to make anyone sink into a numbing depression. Not Mantello. He responded in the only way he considered appropriate and worthwhile–by plunging into intensive efforts to prevent further deaths.

The very night of Manoliu's return, June 20, Mantello was already hard at work. He had read the reports—both the copy of Rosenberg and Wetzler's Auschwitz Protocols and the update on deportations in Hungary, as well as Krausz's plea to Chaim Posner—and had found them shattering. They detailed the cold, systematic murder of over a million and a half Jews at Auschwitz. Mantello was saddened that he hadn't seen the reports earlier. He hadn't expected Rabbi Weissmandl to send him a copy; after all, the two didn't know each other. On the other hand, he had always gone out of his way to share all information at his disposal with other Jewish aid groups. Still, none of them had bothered to tell him about the Weissmandl reports. Neither had they been published in any newspaper. Clearly, they weren't yet receiving the widespread attention they deserved.

Mantello was determined that their contents be publicized throughout the free world. He was certain that no one who read the reports could remain silent about them.

His first step was to have the reports (including Krausz's

letter) translated into English. To this end, he recruited the services of three secretaries who managed to accomplish the task by six o'clock on the morning of June 21. Mantello himself had slightly edited Krausz's letter, sharpening its pleas for assistance and ending it with the words, "Help! Help! Help!"

By then, Mantello had gotten access to a duplicating machine, and he quickly made some fifty copies of the work for immediate distribution. That evening, he met with members of the Association of Swiss Rabbis and the Swiss Committee for Assistance to Hungarian Jews—organizations he had himself organized in 1944—and asked them to publicize the entire package.

However, Mantello did not want to rely on Jews alone to spread the news. Others would only accuse them of self-serving exaggerations. If non-Jews would join the battle, it would supply the reports with enormous credence.

To accomplish this, he met with the Protestant Pastor Paul Vogt, an old acquaintance of his and one of Switzerland's foremost preachers, and convinced him of the reports' authenticity. Then he suggested that Vogt sign an introductory letter that could be sent out with the Protocols.

Vogt had an objection.

"Of course, I'm willing to add my name to such a letter," he told Mantello. "But that alone won't count for especially much. However, if you add the names of other, more prominent Protestant religious leaders, it would attract that much more attention."

And Vogt had some quite specific suggestions about whom to include: Professors Karl Barth, Emil Brunner and Visser t'Hooft, head of the Swiss Ecumenical Council of Churches, all of them internationally known clergymen, the mention of whose names would win the reports widespread publicity.

Mantello wasn't quite sure. There simply wasn't time to

show each of these prominent men the reports and obtain their written consent to being mentioned.

Finally, he decided to take a chance. He drafted a letter, which read as follows: "We are sending two reports from Hungary with an accompanying letter of June 19, 1944, which came via diplomatic channels to Switzerland from a highly reliable source. These reports have profoundly shaken us. Due to our deep sense of responsibility, we feel obligated to make you aware of these two reports. We have no doubt that you will make the effort to read these reports and to spread them among your circles."

And in addition to Vogt's name, he put down those of Drs. Barth, Brunner and t'Hooft, even before he obtained their written permission.

Mantello began circulating the letter, together with the report, and held his breath. Would the Protestant leaders cooperate?

Soon enough, the strict Swiss censorship police—extremely cautious about allowing anything negative to be printed against the Nazis—called Karl Barth and asked if he had given his endorsement to the letter.

Without hesitation, Dr. Barth (who had by now received a copy) shouted, "Well, you see my name there, don't you?"

The other two professors added their agreement in short order. In this way, the Protocols were circulated under the auspices of a very powerful religious Swiss body.

Vogt eventually went even further, publishing within weeks a book called *Am I My Brother's Keeper?*, containing Mantello's reports and other pertinent information. Its powerful condemnation of public indifference to the Jews' fate had a profound effect and gained much sympathy for Jewish refugees in Switzerland.

On June 22, Dr. Zvi Taubes, head of the Association of Swiss Rabbis, met with Monsignor Bernardini, the Vatican's ambassador to Berne who had done much to help the Sternbuchs. Dr. Taubes supplied him with a copy of the reports, and Bernardini immediately sent it off to the Vatican with his recommendation that action be taken in response. A positive reply soon followed.

Fellow diplomats also received copies of the reports from Mantello. Among these was Commodore Freddy West, the British military attache and the highest-ranking intelligence officer in Switzerland. West shared the information with his American colleague Allen Dulles, and although they had known of the Nazi atrocities against Jews, they were flabbergasted at reading how extensive and deliberately cold-blooded the murders at Auschwitz were. They both immediately resolved to send word of the reports to their governments.

One of the few people not stirred by the reports was Roswell McClelland, the American representative of the War Refugee Board in Switzerland. McClelland had tried to block many of the Sternbuchs' rescue initiatives, and now he showed no interest in learning the truth about Auschwitz. When Mihaly Banyai of the Swiss Committee for Assistance to Jews in Hungary asked to meet with him about the situation, McClelland simply said, "I have no need to meet with you." And he never did. Only after the reports had become a major news topic in Switzerland did a still skeptical McClelland agree to send a copy to his superiors in Washington.

Perhaps the one individual who did the most to disseminate copies of the reports was a journalist named Walter Garrett. The director of the British Exchange Telegraph news agency, Garrett had long known and admired Mantello. Still, he was at first reluctant to accept the authenticity of the reports. Could all these appalling things really be true? Was it possible?

Seeking verification, he called his friend Commodore West, the British intelligence officer.

"I know Mantello is a fine fellow," said Garrett. "But is he fully reliable?"

"Let me tell you something about Mr. Mantello," West replied. "I was once looking for a way to send thousands of very valuable Swiss chronographs (precision watches) to England for use by our pilots in the war. That wasn't a simple matter, my friend. The equipment was worth millions, and more important, these valuable instruments are important for our pilots. They are very hard to obtain. Then Mantello agreed to smuggle it out in his Salvadoran diplomatic pouch, and he took care of everything.

"Now, anybody else in that situation would have taken full advantage of it, forcing me to pay plenty in bribe money, you know. But not Mantello. He didn't ask for a shilling. Just did everything I asked, for free. So is he trustworthy? Absolutely no doubt in my mind. If he issues a report, you can be sure it's the truth."

Thus reassured, Garrett set out to disseminate the reports with astonishing speed.

On the evening of June 23, Garrett sent abbreviated versions of the reports, in the form of four cables, to a wide variety of world leaders. These included President Roosevelt, British Prime Minister Winston Churchill, British Foreign Minister Anthony Eden, the Archbishop of Canterbury and Queen Wilhelmina of Holland.

That very same night, Garrett bicycled around the blacked-out streets of Zurich, Switzerland, delivering copies of the reports to the offices of all major Swiss and foreign newspapers. He had taken care to avoid the restrictions of Swiss censorship against having anti-Nazi newspaper articles originating in Switzerland, by having the reports datelined: Ankara, Turkey.

Garrett then joined Mantello in waiting and hoping for the world to react.

For once, it did.

THE INTERNATIONAL FIRESTORM

One of the first to respond to the blitz of letters and cables was Pope Pius XII. Up to this point, the Pope had been conspicuous for his public silence in regard to the Nazi atrocities against the Jews. Although he was always well aware of what was happening to them, he had not even mentioned the word Jew in his vague call for an end to human suffering. On June 25, though, under prodding by letters from the Protestant leaders, he appealed directly to Hungarian leader Admiral Horthy to "do everything in your power to save as many unfortunate people as possible from further pain and sorrow."

Horthy, a Christian, could not ignore the Pope's message. He replied that "I shall do everything I can to enforce the claims of Christian and humane principles." But action was not immediately forthcoming.

The day after the Pope's missive was sent, President Roosevelt had Secretary of State Cordell Hull issue a sharp warning to Horthy: "Hungary's fate will not be like that of any other civilized nation . . . unless the deportations are stopped . . . I rely not only on words, but also on the force of weapons."

In England, Foreign Minister Anthony Eden likewise condemned the deportations and issued a public declaration that those who took part in them would be punished.

On July 2, Budapest was the target of a massive American air attack. Whether or not this was in response to the deportations isn't clear, but Horthy understood it to mean that the President would stand by his word.

Beginning to waver under the pressure, Horthy assembled his Crown Council and told them, "I shall not tolerate this any further! I shall not permit the deportations to bring further shame on Hungary!"

Still, there was no final decision on the matter, and the international pressure mounted. Cardinal Seredi of Hungary wrote a letter condemning the deportations, and Sweden's King Gustav appealed to Horthy "in the name of humanity, to take steps in favor of those of this suffering people who can still be saved."

Now the press campaign launched by Garrett began to bear fruit, as Swiss newspapers weighed in with strong denunciations of the mistreatment of Jews. Up to this point, the Swiss press had mostly downplayed stories of Nazi abuse of Jewish victims. This was partly due to government-ordered restrictions, as the Swiss tried mightily not to upset their German neighbors. Now, though, with German armies losing the upper hand in the war, the press unleashed a barrage of anti-Nazi stories, no holds barred. Headlines like "Murder of the Innocents," "A Cry of Pain Fills the World" and "For Such a Crime There Can Be No Neutrality" blared forth from the front pages.

The news reports aroused such public wrath that there were protest demonstrations in the streets, led by labor and women's groups. In quiet Switzerland, this was considered very rare.

Mantello took full advantage of all this. Every other day, he sent copies of these published protests to the German Embassy in Bern, Switzerland. To each parcel he attached a written note, warning that the Nazis would be held accountable for their crimes against the Jews.

"You will pay for this!" he wrote again and again.

The Germans vehemently protested the articles and called for an end to the complaints. However, the Swiss government warned them not to censor the reports, or else Swiss sentiment against the Nazis would be further inflamed.

FORCED TO RESPOND

The gist of the information in the reports was soon being reported by much of the world's news media, and this created a furor. The international outcry was such that even the Nazis were pressed to respond publicly.

The Deputy Chief of the German Propaganda Ministry, Helmut Sundermann, held a news conference in which he denied the atrocities attributed to the Nazis. "Why only the other day," he declared, "the Red Cross visited our camp at Thereisienstadt and saw just how humanely all the Jews are treated there."

Most of the world knew better by now.

Finally, Admiral Horthy decided he could no longer abide the international pressure. On July 7, he convened his council and began the meeting by sacking two pro-Nazi ministers Lsazlo Baky and Laszlo Endre. He had discovered that they were plotting to unseat him and install a Nazi-backed government instead.

Then he made an additional announcement. The deportations of the Jews would cease immediately.

The mad rush to slaughter all of Hungary's Jews was finally over. In truth, the Hungarian Jews were not yet totally safe from harm. The vicious goons of Hungary's pro-German Arrow Cross continued to accost and kill Jews in the street. And the Nazis kept trying to send Jews to Auschwitz, occasionally succeeding to a limited extent. But by now, Raoul Wallenberg and representatives of five neutral countries were on the scene, helping thwart their efforts.

In short, the mass deportations stopped and remained suspended for the duration of the war. As a result, over one hundred thousand Jews were still alive in Budapest when the war came to an end.

In addition to sparing these precious lives, the Mantello initiative also effected other major developments.

Enraged by the reports about Auschwitz, the Swedish King not only expressed his opposition to Horthy but also dispatched Raoul Wallenberg to Hungary to assist in rescuing the remaining Jews. During the last year of the war, Wallenberg performed legendary feats of rescue, endangering his own life by offering "official protection" to as many Jews as he could. Along with Swiss and Spanish diplomats, Wallenberg set up "safe houses" where thousands of Jews spent the remainder of the war, secure from Nazi treachery.

The public outrage fanned by the Protocols also awakened the International Red Cross to its duty and led it to work actively on behalf of Jewish war victims for the first time. In Switzerland, the government finally rethought its harsh policy barring Jewish refugees and officially granted them the right to enter.

One man had ignited a spark, and the resulting firestorm had scorched the Nazis' bloody hands.

APPRECIATING A HERO

George Mantello's concern for the Holocaust's victims did not cease when the war ended. In the post-war years, he concentrated on restoring the physical and spiritual health of the survivors, including the Satmar Rebbe, who had lost his entire family during the war. Mantello gave of his personal funds to these individuals and helped restore them to relative well-being. He also helped build Hadar Yosef in Israel, a housing settlement for wounded soldiers outside Tel Aviv.

Throughout his rescue efforts, Mantello had shunned the limelight, never seeking the glory some men crave. Unfortunately, that led to his remarkable work being overlooked and forgotten by many Jews. There was hardly any acknowledgment that this businessman and diplomat had accomplished so much, and he settled in Italy after the war, out of the public eye, to a quiet life with his family.

Then, when he was already in his eighties, attempts to correct the oversight finally began. First, there was a ceremony in his honor in Israel, attended by many of those who owed their survival to him. A similar event occurred in New

York in 1989, when he received a public tribute from Mayor Edward Koch and many other Jewish notables. In 1990, there was a five-minute ovation on his behalf as he received an honorary doctorate from Yeshiva University.

One of the most moving tributes to Mantello came in the summer of 1988 when he attended a major gathering of Holocaust historians in Oxford, England. Despite his age (eighty-eight) and frail health, he remained mentally vigorous and a still-proud member of the Jewish community.

As part of their program honoring Mantello, the organizers of the event had prepared a surprise for him. He was brought face-to-face for the first time with Walter Rosenberg, one of the two men who escaped from Auschwitz and wrote the Auschwitz Protocols. Mantello and Rosenbeg had corresponded with each other but had never before met. It was an emotional moment, as the man who had first described the horrors of Auschwitz and challenged the world to do something about them embraced the man who had been bold enough to take up the challenge and stop the transports to hell.

Everyone watching knew they were indeed in the presence of someone special, someone who had given the lie to the words "It can't be done."

THE SWISS CONNECTION

MRS. RECHA STERNBUCH

Recha Sternbuch was a Jewish housewife who braved opposition by assimilated Jews, danger and arrest, to personally organize a smuggling ring to bring in hundreds of "illegal" Jews from Austria and occupied France into Switzerland. She later became one of the most effective rescue activists, even dealing directly with Himmler, to help rescue many thousands of Jews.

5   THE SWISS CONNECTION

MRS. RECHA STERNBUCH

IT WAS NEARLY MIDNIGHT ON A CLOUDY NIGHT IN SWITZERLAND in 1938, but Mrs. Recha Sternbuch was still awake. Her attention was focused on the telephone. The call she was awaiting would not be a simple friendly chat. Instead, it would bring her word on the fate of a dozen fellow Jews. And it was already hours overdue.

The twelve men, women and children were to be the latest in a long line of Jews given aid by Mrs. Sternbuch and her co-workers. The day before, these twelve people had slipped away from their homes in Germany and been hidden behind the false back of a truck. Then they had been driven to the border between Germany and Switzerland and given instructions on how to sneak across.

That had taken them out of Nazi territory, but they were not yet secure by any means. True, Switzerland was a neutral country, but it was wedged among Nazi-occupied or pro-Nazi countries. Because Switzerland itself had not been invaded by Nazi troops, its Jews lived in relative safety. However, there were many Swiss–including quite a few Jews–who were opposed to any influx of Jewish refugees, even if these were on the run for their lives. They did not want their country flooded with foreigners beholden to strange customs, nor did they wish to be burdened with their support. As a result, the Swiss government, rather than encouraging the arrival of such refugees, tried hard to intercept them. Those caught entering were arrested and, in many cases, returned to the Nazis. Needless to say, such Jews were in dire peril.

To counter this indifference to their fate, Mrs. Sternbuch had helped create a network of smugglers. Through bribes, political connections and astounding acts of daring, the network was often able to sneak the refugees into Switzerland right past the border guards. Yet, the success rate was far from perfect, and each failure gnawed at Mrs. Sternbuch's heart.

This was why she insisted that she be kept posted on the progress of each incoming group. If they were safe, she wanted to help them reach their final destination as quickly as possible. And if they faced danger, she wanted to deal with the problem in any way she could. But this time, there had been no word at all. Now she waited, hoping for the best, fearing the worst.

Then a sharp jangle startled her from her thoughts. She picked up the phone receiver immediately.

"Is everything going according to plan?" she asked.

The voice of her contact person at the other end was low and mournful. "No. The news is not good. The group was across the border, and they'd almost made it to safety. But then the guards spotted them. We tried to come to the rescue, but it was no use."

"Where are they now?"

"The Swiss guards turned them over to the Nazis. They're in a border prison now–in the hands of the Gestapo." The contact person sighed deeply. "We came so close, but now it's hopeless."

"Don't say that. We've worked out problems before."

"But not when they're as bad as this. You don't expect the Nazis to let them go, do you?"

"When you trust in Heaven, nothing's impossible," said Mrs. Sternbuch. "We've got to get them free, even if it means negotiating with the Gestapo directly."

The contact cut her short. "Don't even consider it. They'll lock you up, too, and we can't afford to lose you."

"Don't worry about me. I have political connections; I can take care of myself. But who will help these poor Jews if we don't? Time is wasting. We have to get to work."

The contact person tried to talk her out of her wild plan, but her mind was already made up. As soon as she had received all the available information about the case, Mrs. Sternbuch was on her way to the border. Riding along in the pitch blackness, she felt her heart thumping wildly. She had faced danger before, but this time she was heading straight into the mouth of the Nazi monster itself. Yet, her prayers were not for her own safety but for that of the twelve trapped Jews.

Suddenly, she heard warning shots whizzing above her, and then shouts of "Halt!" She kept going. Next, floodlights blazed in her eyes. Four border guards materialized beside her, ordering her to stop.

"Where are you going?" they demanded. "What do you want here?"

For a moment, she was too stunned to reply. Then she found her voice, and it was surprisingly firm and forceful. "I have an important matter to discuss with your prison chief," she said. "I must see him at once."

Her confident manner convinced the guards that she must be someone important. Instead of challenging her, they brought her to the border prison, which was surrounded by other guards as well as snarling dogs. As she entered, flanked by soldiers, she glimpsed the Jews she'd come to save. They were huddled forlornly in a prison cell in the back.

"Who are *you*?" came a booming voice aimed at her like a gunshot.

She looked up to see the Gestapo chief, a fat sinister man with a vicious attack dog at his feet. "What do you think you're doing in this area?"

Recha Sternbuch summoned up her courage and drew closer. "I am a Swiss citizen," she announced. "Those in the Swiss government know me well. The people you have locked up came to Switzerland under my supervision. I am responsible for their safety. I ask that you turn them over to me."

"What!" The head Nazi roared with the force of a hurricane. "How *dare* you tell me what to do, you filthy dog? You say you have protection? I'll rip up your papers in a minute. Then I'll lock you up with the others and let you rot. So you'd better get out of here while you still can!"

She did not budge. "I will not leave without them," was her clear reply. "If you don't give them to me, I will join them in jail voluntarily. Then, when the Swiss police come looking for me, you'll find yourself in deep trouble."

The two stared at each other, the daring Jewish woman and the Nazi bully. There was a charged silence. Even the guards tensed. Then the Gestapo leader spoke.

"Crazy! A crazy woman!" he shouted. "You must be insane to come here. I should have had you shot the moment you walked in."

He glanced towards the prisoners and then whirled back to the woman before him.

"All right!" he screamed. "Go! Go and take your twelve miserable Jews with you. They're stinking up my headquarters. Get them out of here—quickly!—before I change my mind and kill the whole filthy lot of you."

Recha Sternbuch didn't wait around for any chance of that happening. To their amazement, the Jews watched as the prison doors were opened. Then they were ordered out. As they hurried to comply, they began thanking the woman who had come to rescue them. She just shook her head.

"Save your thanks for Hashem, and your strength for the trip ahead," she told them.

When he learned that the group had indeed been set free, the contact person was astounded.

"How did you do it?" he asked Mrs. Sternbuch. "You must be a miracle worker."

"Hashem performs the miracles," she replied. "I'm only one of His agents. I just carry out my tasks."

And what a Divine agent she was! Her "tasks" included saving and caring for thousands of Jews both during and after the war. And she achieved her successes with a minimum of publicity, and an uncommon abundance of *Ahavas Yisrael*.

A HOTEL AT HOME

Recha Sternbuch's upbringing had instilled in her a devout dedication to acts of *chessed*. She was born in 1905, the fifth child of Rabbi and Mrs. Mordechai Rottenberg. When she was still very young, her family moved from Galicia to Antwerp, Belgium, where her father served as the Chief Rabbi of the Orthodox Jewish community. He was also a member of the Moetzes Gedolei Hatorah, the supreme rabbinical advisory board of Agudath Israel.

Through personal example, he and his wife conveyed to their children a love of Torah learning and a sense of responsibility towards others. Their house was always open to visitors seeking shelter, food or advice. This had a lasting impact on the young Recha, as later events amply proved.

In Yitzchak Sternbuch she met a most suitable mate. The same year that Recha was born, the Sternbuch family moved from Rumania to Switzerland. As one of the few Chassidic families there, they were notably conspicuous, and some of their less religious neighbors were initially suspicious of them. But the Sternbuchs soon won them over through their warm hospitable ways. Among those who stayed at the Sternbuch home during the period of World War I was the great Rabbi Chaim Ozer Grodzensky of Vilna.

When Yitzchak and Recha Sternbuch married and established their own household in St. Gallen, and later in Montreux, Switzerland, they, too, went out of their way to help their neighbors. Tragically, the Jews of Switzerland would soon have to cater to many needy European Jews, and the Sternbuchs' aid was to become increasingly indispensable.

In March, 1938, Germany annexed Austria. Immediately afterwards, the Nazis ordered Jews to be expelled from parts of Austria that their families had called home for centuries. Many Jews sought refuge in neighboring Switzerland, but the Swiss policy, as we have seen, was to deter such moves. In order to keep the Swiss door firmly bolted against these aliens, the government asked the Nazis to identify all Jews under their auspices by placing the letter J on their passports. Jewish adults under the age of sixty who were caught sneaking into Switzerland were handed over to the Gestapo.

"This can't go on," Recha Sternbuch resolved. "Jews can't be treated like runaway slaves being returned to their masters."

She and other concerned individuals therefore established a secret network, consisting of humane Swiss citizens—policemen, taxi drivers, farmers and others. Their goal was to enable Jews to evade governmental barriers and reach safety in Switzerland. The exact roles of the network members were individualized. Some were assigned to make contact with endangered Jews in Germany and help them prepare for departure. Others had the task of spiriting these Jews across the border in camouflaged cars and trucks. Once inside Switzerland, the refugees were usually brought to the Sternbuch home, where they would rest up after their hazardous journey and be given food, clothing and heimishe comfort.

Yet, they were still subject to arrest, since they had entered the country illegally. To remain, they needed official recognition of their new status, or a visa if they wished to depart elsewhere. Recha Sternbuch was once again well-equipped to meet these needs. Some time earlier, she had made the acquaintance of Paul Gruninger, the local Chief of Police. He wasn't Jewish, but he was a bitter foe of the Nazis. When Mrs. Sternbuch told him how her fellow Jews were being brutalized in Germany, he agreed to join her crusade. "I'll do anything to help anyone escape those Nazi barbarians," he declared.

And so, working behind the scenes with Mrs. Sternbuch's group, he attempted to grant legal Swiss residency to all the Jewish refugees who needed it. In many cases, he was notably successful. Some Jews were able to remain safely in the country, while others stayed only until they could get as far away from Europe as possible. Mrs. Sternbuch and others helped many gain access to Eretz Yisrael through illegal transports that thwarted British obstacles to their arrival.

Whatever their situation, though, the refugees enjoyed the reassuring hospitality of the Sternbuchs' home. "When I first came to live with you, I was positive I was being put up in a hotel, not a private family home," one of the refugees later told the Sternbuchs. "But then I realized that even hotels don't treat their guests so hospitably."

BEYOND THE CALL OF DUTY

Yet, with all this, Recha Sternbuch still wasn't satisfied. She constantly felt the driving need to do more.

"You're doing plenty," her friends assured her. "No one who comes here could possibly ask for better care. Besides, you have so many other things to keep you busy. There's your household and your children, not to mention the business. Isn't that enough? You can't do everything."

"Saving lives *is* everything!" she answered. "How can I ever raise my children properly if I don't show them that? What will I ever say to them when they ask me one day what I was doing while the Nazis were terrorizing our people? The business can wait, the refugees can't."

Her immediate concern was that many Jews seeking escape were stymied by lack of a visa. Soon, she hit upon a plan of action. She began making frequent, potentially perilous trips to Germany and Austria, carrying and distributing the precious visas she'd obtained through her contacts. Among those whose release she secured there were even several inmates of the Dachau concentration camp. Mrs. Sternbuch also spent several months in Italy during 1938-9, securing visas that would let refugees in Switzerland travel to Eretz Yisrael via Italy.

Eventually, her husband Yitzchak and her brother-in-law Eli were caught up in her enthusiasm and likewise became increasingly active in rescue work. This led to a corresponding neglect of the family business and a significant financial loss. Nevertheless, the Sternbuchs' devotion to *hatzalah* kept growing.

SUPPORT FROM UNEXPECTED SOURCES

For all she accomplished, Recha Sternbuch never sought the limelight and shied away from public credit for herself. Instead, she went out of her way to praise all the others who worked alongside her to rescue Jews. These included several righteous gentiles, such as Police Chief Paul Gruninger, who has already been mentioned; Alexander Lados, the Polish government-in-exile's Ambassador to Switzerland; and the Pope's representative in Bern, Switzerland, Monsignor Philippe Bernardini. They all became Mrs. Sternbuch's allies, in part because she always sought help from any available source, however unlikely.

Ambassador Lados aided her in numerous ways. Through his Jewish assistant Dr. Julius Kuhl, he issued hundreds of Polish passports to stateless Jews who would otherwise have been arrested and deported. Among those who gained a passport in this manner was the sainted Belzer Rebbe, Rabbi Aharon Rokeach. Dr. Kuhl was instrumental in the Rebbe's escape to Eretz Yisrael, which succeeded despite the Nazis' furious search for him.

The Ambassador also helped the Sternbuchs secure kosher food for Jewish refugees held in Swiss detention camps and protected Jews in army bases from mistreatment. (He showed his disdain for such bias by having his Jewish aid Dr. Kuhl represent him at meetings with army brass.) Perhaps most important of all, he allowed the Sternbuchs to use his office for sending confidential, uncensored messages to the free world through the Polish diplomatic pouch, an act that would otherwise have been virtually impossible during wartime. Through this vehicle, the Sternbuchs were later able to alert American Jews to the incredible horrors of the death camps. "Without Mr. Lados's help, hardly any Jews at all would have gained a haven in Switzerland," the Sternbuchs later wrote.

The Sternbuchs made the acquaintance of Monsignor Bernardini through Dr. Kuhl. At their first formal encounter, Mrs. Sternbuch asked Bernardini for a letter of recommendation that she might use as a reference when meeting other personages. The Church leader asked her what she wished the letter to state, and then wrote down her exact response, word for word.

"Why are you doing all this for me?" she asked in pleased astonishment, not used to this level of accommodation. "After all, you don't even know me."

"I have been a diplomat for a long time now," the Monsignor explained, "and I've learned to tell who is honest and who isn't. From the way you've acted since you entered my office, and the obvious strength of your religious convictions, I could tell you were sincere. That's why I'm more than willing to help you."

Months later, after coming to appreciate Mrs. Sternbuch's work even more fully, he told her, "You can call me for help whenever you want, day or night, and I'll answer."

Monsignor Bernardini's gracious assistance came in a variety of forms. Due to his superior diplomatic rank, government officials paid respectful heed to his suggestions. Therefore, when there was an urgent need to release Jews from Swiss detention camps or to gain legal recognition for questionable passports, the Monsignor's intervention proved most effective.

At one point, the Swiss government allowed entire families with young children to enter Switzerland as refugees. However, at the same time they refused admission to single individuals between the ages of sixteen and sixty. Mrs. Sternbuch could not let such a policy go unchallenged. Therefore, when she was preparing the refugees for admission to Switzerland, she simply included these single individuals as members of existing families.

Eventually, the Swiss authorities discovered what was happening, and they were livid. The Swiss were especially offended by lies, and they felt they'd been deceived in this case. As a result, they threatened to block all future Jewish immigration to the country.

In desperation, Mrs. Sternbuch sought Monsignor Bernardini's help. He acted swiftly, speaking to government officials about the matter and delivering a radio address about it. Yes, he told the Swiss public, lying was wrong. But it was understandable and even necessary in this situation, when lives might otherwise very likely be lost. By clarifying the priorities involved, Monsignor Bernardini appeased the Swiss people and soothed the government officials. As a result, the refugees involved were allowed to remain in Switzerland, and there were no further threats to curtail immigration.

The Sternbuchs were most appreciative of the aid provided by these righteous gentiles, and they openly expressed their profound gratitude to them. After the war, when Mr. Lados was living in lonely retirement, spurned by the Polish Communist leaders, the Sternbuchs maintained a steady correspondence with him and sought to assist him financially. And to thank Monsignor Bernardini for his generous and sympathetic acts, they presented him with a beautiful gift on behalf of the Jewish people.

FAILING THE CHALLENGE

Unfortunately, not everyone was so cooperative. Not even certain Jews.

By 1939, Switzerland was inhabited by some 19,000 Jews, most of whom desired to live as quietly and unobtrusively as possible. They remembered the recent, bitter years of anti-Jewish sentiment, when Swiss Jews had found it difficult to secure jobs and *shechitah* had been banned. As a result, they felt that attracting attention to themselves might jeopardize their newly-won rights and entry into Swiss society. If they minded their business and remained quiet law-abiding citizens, they felt, they would remain safe and could continue on the road to full social acceptance. On the other hand, if they actively pressed the government to take in Jewish refugees, the strange newcomers might engender renewed religious persecution and bar further attempts at assimilation.

These "modern" Swiss Jews didn't want to be associated with the "backwards" Orthodox aliens. Therefore, there was no great outcry among Swiss Jews for their country to take in Jewish refugees. Besides, amid the tranquil beauty of their surroundings, it was easy for Swiss Jews to overlook the terror raging just across the border.

One Swiss Jew who staunchly promoted these views was Mr. Saly Mayer, a retired manufacturer who was probably the single most influential Jew in Switzerland. Mayer happened to be a good friend of Dr. Heinrich Rothmund, the head of the Swiss Alien Police, assigned to stop refugees at the border. It had, in fact, been Rothmund who had suggested to the Nazis that they stamp Jewish passports with a large J, to aid in identifying and dooming them. Both Mayer and Rothmund were in agreement that accepting Jewish refugees would not be in Switzerland's best interests. They did not pause to consider what was in the best interests of these Jews.

Nevertheless, when an emergency arose that required concessions from the government, Mrs. Sternbuch turned to Saly Mayer. She was sure he would put his close ties to Rothmund to good use for the benefit of his fellow Jews.

"Mr. Mayer, I come to you today as a Swiss Jewish woman, to ask for your help. The situation requires it."

"Just what are you referring to, Mrs. Sternbuch?"

"A recent border event. Two Jewish brothers were caught trying to enter Switzerland. The Swiss police are threatening to turn them over to the Nazis, and they'll probably rot away in a concentration camp if that happens. We have to act quickly if we're to save them. Could you possibly contact Dr. Rothmund and ask him to intervene?"

Saly Mayer nodded grimly. "Yes, I know all about the case of the two brothers. And I've already decided what should be done."

"Good. Then if you could alert me when you've managed to win their release."

"Excuse me, Mrs. Sternbuch. What I meant was, I've decided that nothing can or *should* be done to free them."

Recha Sternbuch, who took certain moral imperatives for granted, couldn't believe what she was hearing.

"Let me set you straight," Mayer continued. "We Swiss Jews have to be very careful. We have to follow our country's laws to the letter; our enemies are just waiting for us to trip up. Now, if these brothers broke the law, they'll have to pay the price. If they entered Switzerland illegally, they must be returned to the place from where they came. Otherwise, there will be a big hubbub, and we Jews can't afford the bad publicity.

"And while I'm on the subject, let me tell you another thing. I know you've been very active in bringing refugees to Switzerland, Mrs. Sternbuch. I understand your views, and I can sympathize with them. But I'm not so sure you're doing your fellow Jews a service. The Swiss have been treating us tolerably well lately, and as long as we don't make waves, everything will remain fine. But if we start bringing in all these foreigners—especially those with the long beards and black hats—we're just asking for trouble.

"We Jews shouldn't stand out in the crowd, should we? That will only bring a return of the black days when we were social outcasts. And I'm sure neither you nor I wants to cause that. Am I right?"

Mrs. Sternbuch stared at him for a moment as she struggled to control the rage surging through her. "I'm so sorry that the sight of too many Jews repels you, Mr. Mayer," she shot back. "I am not ashamed of helping my fellow Jews come to this country, even if it unsettles our gentile neighbors. I consider it my duty to aid these Jews in their time of need. I only worry that if we wait too long, there won't be any Jews left to help.

"Now, if it means I have to bend the law a little at times to save a life and if this makes some other Jews uncomfortable, well, Mr. Mayer, that is just too bad."

"In that case," he responded, "I'm afraid that I can't help

you, Mrs. Sternbuch."

"Then I will just have to continue the rescue work without you, Mr. Mayer. Good day."

With that, Recha Sternbuch rose and marched out of Saly Mayer's office, never to return.

THE AUTHORITIES CRACK DOWN

Despite her stormy confrontation with Mayer, Mrs. Sternbuch did not abandon her rescue attempts. In fact, she solidified her resolve and quickened her pace of activity. If she was to do without Mayer's help, she would have to work even harder. By the end of 1938, some eight hundred Jewish refugees had been the beneficiaries of the *mitzvah* of *hachnasass orchim* in its fullest sense at the Sternbuch home.

The Sternbuchs knew their efforts were fraught with danger. They knew that not everyone approved of their attitude towards the refugees. What they could not guess was that some of their own fellow Jews would be the ones to almost sink their campaign.

Mrs. Sternbuch discovered this on the day she came to discuss a pressing matter with Paul Gruninger, the ever-helpful chief of police. She sought him in his office and throughout the building but caught no sight of him. Finally, she summoned help.

"I'm looking for Mr. Gruninger. Do you know where I might find him?"

"Not here, that's for sure," she was told. "He was dismissed last week."

When a shocked Recha Sternbuch eventually managed to contact him at his home, Gruninger explained the circumstances of his dismissal.

"You can thank Saly Mayer for what happened," he said. "According to what I've found out, he didn't like all these

Jewish refugees filtering into Switzerland. So one of his assistants filed a report giving details of how I'd helped illegal immigrants stay in the country. Nobody asked for such a report; there was no need to write it. But a copy was sent to Rothmund, and it gave him a perfect excuse to get rid of me. As if I were guilty of some horrendous crime, like spying for the enemy. Still, I don't regret what I've done for those refugees, and I never will. If we're all going to be heartless, what's the point of fighting the Nazis?"

The Sternbuchs saw to it that his selflessness did not go unrecognized. When Gruninger came upon hard times, they secured a job for him and did everything they could to bolster his spirits. Finally, in 1968, he was honored by Yad Vashem, the Israeli Holocaust Museum and Archives. A tree was planted in his honor in the Avenue of Righteous Gentiles—a long overdue tribute. The resulting publicity led to his being given, at long last, the pension he had forfeited upon being unjustly fired.

When interviewed after the war, Gruninger claimed that if all Swiss Jews had supported the rescue work—and especially if some influential Jews hadn't actively opposed it—an additional ten to twenty thousand Jews might have been able to escape the Nazis via Switzerland.

Soon Recha Sternbuch, too, had to face the wrath of the authorities.

In the spring of 1939, she responded to a sharp knock at her door.

"Are you Recha Sternbuch?" a man in military dress demanded.

She nodded.

"Then I've come to arrest you," he continued.

She was stunned. "On what grounds?"

"Smuggling illegal aliens into the country and bribing public officials. Please come with me."

She was formally arraigned and then locked up in prison,

where she remained like a common criminal for two weeks. It was an especially agonizing time for her, not only because the conditions in jail were so degrading but also because she couldn't be at home attending to her refugees. The possibility that her rescue work might have to end altogether caused her the most anguish of all.

Finally, her case came to trial. The prosecutor grilled her about her role in shepherding aliens into Switzerland and paying off border guards to look the other way. Time and again, he pounded away at the question. "Who helped you in this work? Who drove the refugees across the border? We want to know names."

Mrs. Sternbuch's resolve never wavered. "Yes, it's true that I cared for immigrants who came to my home. I also paid for them to be transported to other homes and took care of their debts. You see, I couldn't let these poor people suffer or be turned over to the murderers. Yes, I admit all that.

"But there is one thing I will not do, and that is to inform on others. I've always believed that when innocent perse- cuted people beg for help, I should give it, and that if there are consequences for this, that I should face them. So I'm ready to spend the rest of my life in prison, if necessary. I don't mind being punished, if that is my fate for saving lives. But I will never knowingly get others in trouble. So don't ask me to inform on anyone; that's something I will never lower myself to do. I'll leave that to the Nazis and their breed. And if you think you can get me to name names by suggesting a deal, then you just don't know me at all."

She remained steadfast in her stance. The case dragged on for three frustrating years, during which time she remained free but under strict surveillance. Yet, although distressed by the ordeal, Mrs. Sternbuch never wavered in her resolve and never incriminated others. Finally, in June 1942, the judge determined that she had not broken any laws. To the Stern- buchs' relief, not only were all charges against her dropped but the court assumed all costs of the trial.

Surrounded by family and friends, Mrs. Sternbuch stood in court, pleased at the outcome, when she noticed the prosecuting attorney approaching her. Tensing, she asked, "Are there any other problems?"

"No," he said softly. "I just wanted to know if I could give you this."

He handed her a hundred franc note.

Noting her astonishment, he explained, "I prosecuted you because it was my job. Now that the case is over, I can pay personal tribute to a very courageous lady through a small contribution of my own. I hope you'll use the money for your most worthy work."

SHARED EFFORT

That work redoubled as the war began and the Jews' plight deteriorated. In time, the Sternbuchs came to join forces with other *hatzalah* activists and expanded their efforts to reach out to Jews beyond Switzerland. For example, they started shipping food packages to Jews in the ghettoes of Warsaw, Cracow and Lodz, among others. A friend of the Gerrer Rebbe's daughter later recounted how one such package enabled the Rebbe's family to survive for an entire month, for its contents could be exchanged for a large quantity of basic foods. When a typhoid epidemic broke out in the Warsaw Ghetto in late 1940, the Sternbuchs sent medical supplies there, saving many lives in the process.

When the Japanese attacked Pearl Harbor in December, 1941, drawing the United States into the war, a group of several thousand Jews found themselves in an awkward situation. These Jews–including many *rabbonim* and *yeshivah* students, such as the entire student body of the Mirrer Yeshivah–had journeyed from Vilna, Lithuania, to Shanghai,

China, to escape the double threats of Nazi and Russian persecution. In this foreign city, so alien to their customary surroundings, many Jews had managed to maintain a survival remarkably faithful to their traditions; *shmiras hamitzvos* and Torah study continued unabated among the *yeshivah* students. Financial aid had come from the American Joint Distribution Committee, among other Jewish groups in the United States. However, once America entered the war, all communications between the United States and Japan were severed, and aid to the Shanghai-based Jews, who were under Japanese control, was cut off. Unless some alternative funding could be found, these Jews faced starvation.

The Sternbuchs were in a special position to help. Operating out of a neutral nation, they were able to maintain ties with Jews in Japanese-held territory without restrictions. There would be nothing illegal about sending funds from Switzerland to the *yeshivah* community in Shanghai.

Until then, the Sternbuchs had been able to finance most of their rescue operations from their own funds. However, their limited resources could not possibly support the large number of *yeshivah* students in Shanghai. Therefore, they created a special organization that would do so, calling it HIJEFS (a German-language acronym for "Relief Association for Jewish Refugees in Shanghai").

The group's first publicity leaflet read, "Help rescue our starving fellow Jews in Shanghai! Every Jewish heart must respond to this call!" It was signed by Mrs. Recha Sternbuch, and this marked the first and only time her name appeared publicly in connection with HIJEFS. Later, many prominent *rabbonim* and Jewish businessmen would be listed as HIJEFS's sponsors, but not Mrs. Sternbuch, who reverted to her usual role as a behind-the-scenes mover of events.

Special mention must be given to the incredibly dedicated HIJEFS staff, including Herman Landau, Chaskel Rand and Dr. Reuben Hecht, who undertook difficult and often hazardous missions without batting an eyelash. Yet, HIJEFS remained very much a venture of the Sternbuchs. At its inception, HIJEFS's headquarters were housed in the Sternbuchs' dining room. And aside from the Sternbuchs receiving absolutely no pay for their work with HIJEFS, they also saw to it that organizational expenses for travel and phone calls were paid for out of their own pockets.

Eventually, HIJEFS became the Swiss arm of the American Vaad Hatzalah. The Vaad, which had been founded by Rabbi Eliezer Silver in 1939 and which maintained strong ties with Agudath Israel, had as its original goal the procurement of visas and financial aid to the *yeshivah* students stranded in Shanghai. Later, it expanded its services to assist all Jews in Shanghai; and yet later, at the behest of Rabbi Michoel Ber Weissmandl, it broadened its scope to saving Jews throughout Europe. Besides Rabbi Silver, its directors came to include Rabbi Avraham Kalmanowitz and Rabbi Aharon Kotler.

Since the Vaad was an American-based organization, it was prevented by the U.S. government from sending funds directly to Japanese territory. To circumvent this obstacle, the Vaad (largely under Rabbi Kalmanowitz's initiative) developed a method to transfer the money via secret codes to neutral Switzerland. HIJEFS, in turn, sent it to desperate Jews in Shanghai. At first considered illegal, this procedure eventually won the approval of the American government. The working relationship between the Vaad and the Sternbuchs proved singularly effective and harmonious, and through their combined efforts, thousands of imperiled Jews received vital packages of food, clothing and medicine.

After the war, Rabbi Chaim Shmuelevitz, the *rosh yeshivah* of the Mirrer Yeshivah, expressed the gratitude of the entire *yeshivah* community of Shanghai to the selfless HIJEFS staff. "With the help of the Almighty," he wrote, "your self-sacrificing work enabled us to survive the worst of times and to continue our holy task."

Courtesy of Ambassador Lados, the Sternbuchs also used Polish diplomatic couriers to alert the free world to the European Jews' deteriorating situation. (Later, they used the same route to publicize Rabbi Weissmandl's call for Allied bombing of the rail lines to Auschwitz.) Because of their solid ties to the Polish Embassy (which in turn had contact with the Polish underground) and to Mr. J. Domb, a Swiss Jew living in Warsaw, the Sternbuchs learned early of the incredible goals of Hitler's grisly Final Solution. They did not keep the stunning news to themselves.

On September 3, 1942, the Sternbuchs dispatched a cable to Moreinu Yaakov Rosenheim, the President of the Agudath Israel World Organization, in New York, via the Polish diplomatic pouch. It stated that, according to very reliable information at their disposal, the Nazis had already brutally murdered over one hundred thousand Jews in death camps–and that the mass murders were continuing. The cable warned that, unless America took immediate steps against the perpetrators, the murders would go on and on.

Not many shared the Sternbuchs' impatient determination. At this time, Americans generally felt that claims of mass murders approaching the hundreds of thousands were gross exaggerations. The Nazis, cruel as they were, simply could not be *that* inhuman.

Thus, when Stephen Wise of the American Jewish Congress received a similar cable from Gerhardt Riegener, the Congress's Geneva representative, a few days earlier, he did not immediately publicize it or use it as a springboard for action. Instead, he passed it on for confirmation to the U.S. State Department, which held it for ten full weeks. In the meanwhile, Wise ordered all Jewish organizations to remain quiet about the report while it was being confirmed.

Yet, Moreinu Yaakov Rosenheim and Rabbi Kalman-, owitz who had received a similar communication from them, trusted the Sternbuchs and accepted their word at face value.

As a result, they convened a meeting of Jewish leaders, and pressed hard for concrete action. In addition, Moreinu Rosenheim sent a cable to President Roosevelt, requesting an urgent meeting to discuss the tragic situation. He hoped that if the President gained a clear perspective on the extent of the Nazis' crimes, he would be roused from his indifference towards Jewish rescue efforts.

The Rosenheim cable was never answered.

THE PASSPORT PLAN

Catering to needy refugees, gaining official protection for aliens, dispensing funds and supplying food to Jews stranded throughout the world–she was immersed in all these efforts. Yet, Recha Sternbuch was not about to rest on any laurels. She was restless and unsatisfied. There was more she could do. Much more.

"We try, and sometimes we manage to help a few Jews here and there," she fretted, "but the Nazis are killing off whole communities, whole civilizations, and no one tries to stop them. What good is sending food packages to Jews when there are no Jews left to receive them?"

Pursuing this line of logic, she concluded that the scope of her projects had to be expanded. Just what could be done to aid the masses of needy Jews in Europe was not easy to determine. The Sternbuchs held brainstorming sessions with their co-workers, but most of the resulting ideas proved impractical. Then, seemingly out of nowhere, a plan of action presented itself.

One day, one of the Sternbuchs' contacts made a chance remark that sparked a new venture. "I just heard something strange that happened in Poland. It seems the Nazis were making mincemeat of a small Polish town, arresting Jews left and right. But somehow, there was one Jewish man who remained untouched during the whole rampage. Not only didn't the Nazis manhandle him, but they even treated him with respect."

"Respect?" The Sternbuchs were dumbfounded. "The Nazis showing respect to a Jew? Did he bribe them?"

"Apparently not. It seems that he had something else going for him."

"What do you mean?"

"Somehow, he'd gotten a Latin American passport from one of his relatives overseas. He showed it to the Nazis and declared that he was under foreign protection. And when the Nazis heard that, they backed off. They didn't want to get involved with any diplomatic hassles, I guess."

The Sternbuchs looked at each other.

"Do you think it can work again?" Mrs. Sternbuch asked her husband.

"It's certainly worth a try."

Their agenda was now clear-cut, but implementing it was hardly simple. The first step was to secure as many Latin American passports as possible, a task complicated by the fact that the papers costs hundreds of dollars each. Then came the risky job of ensuring that the papers reached the hands of those for whom they were intended. Any slip-ups, and at the very least, the papers would vanish; more seriously, the messenger delivering the papers might face the Nazis' wrath.

Nevertheless, the program proved to be a worthy one. The Nazis continued to treat those who possessed the Latin American papers as special cases. Instead of expelling or killing them, the Nazis either left them untouched or sent them to special detention camps which lacked many of the brutal features of the concentration camps. Apparently, the Nazis acted in this way not out of any love for these Jews, but to ensure that the many thousands of German citizens in Latin America would similarly be treated properly.

Among those who benefitted from these papers, and

who were interned at such preferred detention camps like Vittel and Tittmoning in France, were Recha Sternbuch's own parents.

At the end of 1943, though, events took an ominous turn. The Nazis suddenly began questioning the validity of the Latin American papers. This occurred when they saw they would not be able to exchange the holders of these papers for German citizens living elsewhere. As a result, the Jews who had formerly felt protected were now subject to the same harsh treatment as the others.

On the day after *Pesach*, 1944, a round-up of the Jews at the Vittel detention camp began. Their relatively tranquil existence abruptly gave way to a brutal life at the Drancy concentration camp near Paris.

The Sternbuchs eventually learned of these developments, to their great alarm. Their worst fears were being played out. With frenzied effort, they tried to get the Latin American countries to declare the documents held by the Jews to be valid. If this happened, the Nazis might rethink their position and once again leave these Jews unharmed.

To accomplish this, they dispatched letter after letter and cable after cable to diplomats throughout the world. The Sternbuchs reached out to all their varied contacts, including Ambassador Lados and Monsignor Bernardini, and begged them to intercede. Somehow, *something* had to be done.

The barriers to be surmounted were formidable. To succeed, the Sternbuchs had to get the Latin American countries to verify their legal recognition of the papers; then get the Spanish and Swiss representatives in Germany to intervene with the German Foreign Minister in Berlin on the Jews' behalf; and finally, coax the United States to assure Germany that the holders of the Latin American papers might be exchanged for Germans in Allied countries.

All this took an enormous amount of time. The Vaad Hatzalah and Monsignor Bernardini applied pressure on Latin

American countries to certify the papers, and the plan began to fall into place. However, by the time all the necessary details had been ironed out, those in the Vittel camp had been transferred to Auschwitz. All but three of the 238 Vittel Jews were quickly murdered. Included were many of Mrs. Sternbuch's relatives, including her beloved parents.

Mrs. Sternbuch grieved bitterly over her personal loss, as well as the loss of all the other Jews. However, she eventually had the consolation of knowing that Jews elsewhere were indeed spared because their Latin American papers had been recognized. The initiative of the Sternbuchs and Vaad Hatzalah provided the foundation for other rescue efforts centering around the Latin American papers. Foremost among these was that conducted by George Mantello, a venture that led to tens of thousands of Jews being saved in Hungary.

THE STRANGE STORY OF THE KASTNER TRAIN

Towards the end of the war, the Sternbuchs participated in other such gambles, which produced the same mixed results of exhilarating success and crushing disappointments. One of the most momentous of these began with a totally unexpected phone call.

It was March, 1944. The Nazis had just occupied Hungary, the home of a half million Jews. Philip Freudinger, the head of the Orthodox Jewish community in Budapest and a leader of its Jewish Council, was called to the phone.

"This is Dieter Wisliceny speaking," came a crisp voice. "I wish to meet with you."

Mr. Freudinger shuddered.

Yes, he knew that name—it was the same Wisliceny whom Rabbi Weissmandl had dealt with. Freudinger knew him as a Major in the dreaded Nazi SS, a right hand man of the notorious Adolf Eichmann. A call from this odious German undoubtedly meant trouble. But Freudinger was in no position to reject Wisliceny's summons.

When he arrived at the Nazi's office, he found Wisliceny in an oddly agreeable mood. "Please sit down, Mr. Freudinger, and make yourself comfortable. I have something rather important to discuss with you."

Freudinger settled uncertainly in a seat. What was this Nazi up to?

"I have a letter here written by a colleague of yours, a Rabbi Weissmandl," Wisliceny continued.

Freudinger nodded. He had indeed heard of Rabbi Weissmandl's heroic rescue attempts, and the two had met several times.

"The rabbi assumes—correctly, I may add—that now that Hungary is in our hands, Hungarian Jews are in grave danger. He proposes that the Jews be allowed to buy their freedom. What are your feelings about that idea?"

Freudinger wasn't sure if this wasn't a trap. He thought it prudent to stay quiet and let the Nazi speak.

Wisliceny smiled. "I see you are too surprised to answer me. Let me tell you my reaction, then. I think it happens to be a good idea—a very good idea, in fact. You see, we Germans have recently suffered some losses on the battlefield. Our resources are a bit depleted. So, as far as we are concerned, weapons are more important to us than a group of smelly Jews. That is why we might be willing to make a trade. Jews for funds."

Wisliceny watched Freudinger's eyes widen in amazement. "Mind you," he went on, "we are not talking about a few pennies here. We want at least two million dollars from you in order to begin talking business. But since all Jews are supposed to be rich, that shouldn't be much of a problem, should it?"

Freudinger squirmed in his seat. Jews in Nazi-occupied Hungary had very limited access to funds, and he had no idea from where the two million dollars might come. Still, he wanted to keep this promising option wide open. "I will contact my organization," he said, "and I'm sure we can begin negotiations on this in the very near future."

The talks did move forward, and initially they were conducted in a promising atmosphere. The Nazi and the Jews discussed exactly how much money was to be paid and how many Jews would be spared in exchange. Concurrently, Freudinger and others met with Hungarian Jewish business-men to explore ways of securing the money. Based on these discussions, Freudinger arrived at a scheduled meeting with Wisliceny bearing encouraging news.

"The sum of money you asked for will soon be in your hands," he said.

Wisliceny didn't seem impressed. "Too late," he said. "You should have acted sooner. I've gotten tired waiting for you to keep your promises. I'm afraid our conversations are at an end. Good day, Mr. Freudinger."

Freudinger sat still. He was too dazed to react. Finally, he realized that Wisliceny was serious; he was being dismissed. He had no idea what had gone wrong, but there was nothing more he could do. He muttered a "Good day," and left.

Later, he learned what had happened. Another Jewish group, the Socialist Zionists, had nudged their way into the picture. The local Zionist leaders, Rudolph Kastner and Joel Brand, had managed to convince Wisliceny that they could offer him a more substantive deal than the Orthodox Jews. Wisliceny promptly dropped Freudinger and began negotiat-ing with Kastner and Brand instead.

Consequently, the Nazis made Kastner and Brand a specific offer. Upon receiving a sizable sum of money, they would let seven hundred and fifty Hungarian Jews leave the country. (Eventually, Adolf Eichmann himself proposed to Brand a trade of one million Jews for 10,000 trucks. Unfortu-nately, Joel Brand was arrested by the British while seeking approval for the deal by Jewish leaders, and it never progressed further.)

It was left to the Jews involved in the negotiations to decide just which seven hundred and fifty Jews would be allowed to go free. The Zionists prepared a list consisting mainly of Zionist leaders, and Kastner added the names of many of his relatives and friends. Then there were a number of wealthy Jews with hidden valuables who managed to bribe their way onto the list.

At this point, Philip Freudinger learned that the Zionists were having difficulty concluding the deal, and that the Nazis in Hungary were eager for immediate cash payments. Offering them a sizable bribe, he was able to add the names of some eighty Orthodox Jews to the group bound for freedom. Among these were such noted leaders as the Satmar Rebbe, the Debreciner Rebbe and Rabbi Yonasan Steif.

The list kept expanding, until it bulged with some twelve hundred names. Finally, these Jews were told to board a train at Budapest, which departed for what the passengers hoped would be the safety of a land beyond the Nazi empire. However, they were well aware that they had not been allowed to head for Eretz Yisrael. Hitler had promised his strong supporter, the Arab Mufti, Amin el Husseini, that Jews would not be let into the Holy Land.

As the train was leaving, four hundred and fifty additional Jews from a nearby labor camp hopped aboard. The total number of passengers on what was being called the "Kastner Train" was now close to seventeen hundred.

Then the train ran straight into a roadblock.

The Nazis wanted concrete proof that the Jews were able to make good on their part of the deal. They suddenly had the train stopped in its tracks and rerouted to a special section of the Bergen-Belsen camp. "It is not going anywhere," the Nazis announced, "until you Jews start giving us our due."

It was blackmail, pure and simple, but the Jews involved

in the negotiations were in no position to call the Nazis' hand. Instead, they desperately searched for ways of proving to the Germans that the funds would be forthcoming. This was hardly a simple matter. Following the years of battering by the Nazis, the surviving European Jews were practically bereft of resources.

It seemed the Kastner train was facing derailment.

Then a cable suddenly arrived, promising Wisliceny that there were two hundred and fifty trucks and tractors being prepared for delivery to him in Switzerland. It was signed, "Ferdinand Roth."

Rabbi Michoel Ber Weissmandl had come through again.

However, a major problem still remained. The Nazis had been temporarily soothed, but the funding for the vehicles would have to be provided very quickly. And Rabbi Weissmandl, in war-torn Slovakia, was certainly in no position to acquire it.

It was now that the Sternbuchs, acting in tandem with Vaad Hatzalah, assumed a pivotal role in the saga.

Yitzchak Sternbuch stepped into the breach immediately. He personally made every attempt to assemble the funds to pay for the trucks and tractors. But when the sums were totalled up, the amount came to only one hundred and fifty thousand Swiss francs. Much more was needed.

To make up the difference, he again, reluctantly, contacted the only Jew in Switzerland who might have the necessary resources at his disposal—Saly Mayer. The result was predictable.

"I do not deal with murderers in any form," Mayer replied. "Principles are sometimes more important than lives." And, mistakenly under the impression that everyone aboard the Kastner train was Orthodox, and that a majority of them were rabbis, he added, "Besides, I don't see why we should pay so much to rescue a trainload of rabbis. They should be like captains; they should go down with their ship."

Rather than cooperating, Mayer seemed determined to sabotage the deal. He brought the negotiations to the attention of the War Refugee Board representative in Switzerland, Roswell McClelland. Like Mayer, McClelland was totally opposed to any negotiations with the Nazis, even if this meant forfeiting Jewish lives. He did his best to obstruct the conclusion of any deal for those on the Kastner train.

Meanwhile, as expected, the Nazis involved in the matter were growing impatient. Their daily demands of "Where is the money?" implied an impending tragic ending to the story.

Nevertheless, the Sternbuchs would not give up. By appealing to every possible benefactor and contributing all his own remaining funds to the cause, Yitzchak Sternbuch was able to obtain letters of credit for ten tractors, to be delivered to the Nazis in return for the passengers' release.

This had the desired effect. As a result, the Nazis freed some of the Jews on the train—318 out of 1684—and let them depart for Switzerland, six weeks after they'd set out. There they received a tumultuous reception. Even the normally restrictive Swiss government granted these Jews a hearty welcome.

Eventually, the Vaad Hatzalah's pressure prompted a reluctant Saly Mayer to supply the rest of the payment. In response, the Nazis released the remaining Jews in the train. And the seventeen thousand Jews who had been transferred to Austria were also spared consignment to a concentration camp. They, too, survived the war.

THE MUSY MISSION

An even farther-reaching rescue effort took place during the final year of the war, and its implementation made use of all the Sternbuchs' skill and courage.

In September, 1944, not yet aware of the fate that had overtaken them, Recha Sternbuch was still seeking news of the Jews deported from the Vittel camp. To this end, she had gotten in touch with a Catholic woman who was reputed to have inside knowledge of the Nazis' plans. However, the woman indicated that she had no inkling of the Vittel Jews' status.

As Mrs. Sternbuch was about to end the conversation, the woman suddenly added an afterthought. "Now that I think of it, I did hear something about certain Jews who were released from a concentration camp recently. Maybe there's hope for your parents yet, Mrs. Sternbuch."

Mrs. Sternbuch was intrigued. "The Nazis aren't usually so accommodating. Do you have any idea what brought this about?"

"I can't be positive, but I heard rumors that someone paid the Nazis a bribe and got the Jews freed."

Mrs. Sternbuch could barely suppress her excitement. "One final question. Think hard. Do you happen to remember the name of this person?"

"I . . . wait a minute . . . yes! The name was Musy."

Musy! Mrs. Sternbuch fell silent. Yes, she'd heard of Dr. Jean-Marie Musy. He was nothing less than a former President of Switzerland, the very last person she'd have guessed to be concerned with saving Jews. Musy was a staunch right-winger, and many of the articles in his newspaper, *La Jeune*, dripped with anti-Jewish diatribes. In addition, Musy was known to be a Nazi sympathizer and an intimate of Heinrich Himmler, the fiendish head of the Gestapo.

Nevertheless, Mrs. Sternbuch didn't discount the prospect of recruiting Musy for her rescue campaign. Sometimes, she'd found that the most effective help had come from the unlikeliest source. If Dr. Musy had been willing to save a few Jews, for whatever reason (perhaps they were friends of his) then maybe he might agree to assist others, too. At heart, the man might be a humanitarian. She decided to contact him.

At their first meeting, Mrs. Sternbuch came straight to the point. "I think we can help you, Dr. Musy, and I know you can help us."

Musy was baffled. "What in the world are you talking about?"

"Let's face facts. The Nazis are losing the war. They're being pushed back all across the continent. It's just a matter of time before the Americans, the British and the Russians link armies to smash them. And when that happens, anyone who supported the Nazis might be accused of collaboration."

"Are you implying that I am in trouble, Mrs. Sternbuch?"

"You might be," she replied. "On the other hand, if you can prove you helped Jews escape Nazi oppression during the war, then that may well count in your favor."

"Help Jews? What did you have in mind?"

"I understand that you've already won the release of a few Jews from concentration camps. We certainly appreciate that. But why stop there? Millions of Jews might already be dead, but thousands are still alive. Who knows how much longer they can survive in the camps? If you could use your influence to persuade the Nazis to release them, then you will become a true hero to our people, and you'll win the acclaim of the entire civilized world."

The seventy-five-year-old Musy was impressed by Mrs. Sternbuch's arguments and agreed to see what he could do. He wrote to his friend Himmler requesting a meeting, and the Gestapo chief agreed.

This promising turn of events spurred the Sternbuchs to assume a broader perspective towards this mission. "We can't afford to think small here," Mrs. Sternbuch advised. "We don't have time for that. Instead, we have to ask for the ultimate— the release of *all* the Jews still in Nazi hands!"

Through his Nazi sources, Musy learned that there were still more than 300,000 Jews being held in concentration camps throughout Europe. Could these be yanked out of the monster's jaws? Bolstering their hopes with fervent prayers, the Sternbuchs saw off Dr. Musy and his son Benoit, a Swiss Air Force officer, in a Mercedes car that the Sternbuchs had bought them for the all-important meeting with Himmler. On top of the car they had a red cross painted, in the hope that this international symbol would deter Allied bombers from attacking it. With them, the Musys had 60,000 francs, supplied by the Sternbuchs for expenses and bribes.

The first meeting went well. Himmler and his associates seemed interested in the concept of bartering Jewish lives for money. They also told Musy that they would reduce their original demand of twenty million Swiss francs (five million American dollars) to the more manageable sum of five million francs.

The Nazis also had another, equally important request—"good will." They had lately been mauled in the world press for their brutal mistreatment of Jews, thanks to a campaign mounted by George Mantello. Therefore, Himmler was interested in seeing the media carry some favorable publicity to counter the recent negative reports. He was realistic enough to realize that Nazi Germany's time was running out, and he wanted to avoid bearing the full brunt of the world's condemnation after the war.

When Musy brought them word of Himmler's conditions, the Sternbuchs were pleasantly surprised. The demand for favorable mention in the world press didn't trouble them. This involved mere words, not ammunition for Nazi battlefield victories. Undoubtedly, the world would see through these lies anyway. What concerned them more was, once again, the never-ending quest for funds.

The search led to predictable results. Deals were made; hopes were raised; and then possibilities faded away when money proved scarce.

Burned by his earlier experiences, Yitzchak Sternbuch

did not bother to approach Saly Mayer this time. Instead, he used the Polish diplomatic pouch to cable his message to Vaad Hatzalah in New York: "Himmler will release 300,000 Jews at rate of 15,000 a month if we deposit sufficient money in Swiss bank accounts. Extremely urgent that one million dollars be raised!"

Unfortunately, this figure–enormous now, many times more so then when the average person earned $25 a week–was beyond the means of the Vaad Hatzalah. The Vaad had indeed been able to raise and send a million dollars to imperiled European Jews throughout 1944. This made it the second most successful Jewish fund-raising group during the war, behind the far larger Joint Distribution Committee. The accomplishment was an astonishing display of determination by a tiny organization, one that had its sketchy start only five years earlier.

Nevertheless, the fact remained that the Vaad's constituency was comprised largely of impoverished immigrants and that its leadership consisted of older *Rabbonim* who could not be sent scurrying around for money everywhere. Expecting the Vaad's struggling membership to once again contribute a fortune in a very short period was unrealistic. The Vaad tried valiantly to raise the necessary funds, but the results fell short.

Despite this, the Sternbuchs went ahead trying to comply with Himmler's other stipulation. They personally went to newspaper editors to plead for some favorable coverage for the Germans. The editors were understandably shocked: "Here you've always asked us to lambast the Nazis in the strongest terms, and now you want us to write nice things about them?" But when the Sternbuchs explained the cause for their about-face, the editors agreed to cooperate. The Sternbuchs' associates in America accomplished a similar task there. Dr. Reuven Hecht deserves special mention for his yeoman efforts in this matter.

Those efforts finally began to bear fruit. Following a second meeting with Dr. Musy, in early 1945, Himmler ordered the release of twelve hundred Jews from the Thereisienstadt concentration camp. But where were they to go? The Sternbuchs and Vaad Hatzalah spearheaded a campaign to prod the United States, which in turn pressured Switzerland to accept them. Assured that the United States would guarantee the expenses for their upkeep, the Swiss agreed to allow these Jews entry, and they were warmly welcomed by a sizable throng, headed by Swiss President von Steiger himself.

Accompanying the cheers, though, were the usual cautionary warnings. A relatively small number like twelve hundred was acceptable, but would this herald the beginning of a flood of Jewish refugees to Switzerland? The customary opponents of such a development—both Jews and non-Jews—were determined that this would not happen. Himmler had offered to release another one to two thousand Jews every other week if additional money were on its way. Saly Mayer and others worked hard to see to it that it was not. If it were up to him and Roswell McClelland, the Jews would remain in the camps under Red Cross supervision rather than find freedom in Switzerland.

Other problems, too, began to sink the Sternbuch-Musy initiative. While some of the newspapers had followed the Sternbuchs' plea and had praised the Nazis for releasing the twelve hundred Jews, others had balked. Their anti-Nazi articles upset Himmler and his associates and made them reconsider the tactic of negotiating with Jews. At the same time, the Sternbuchs came under severe criticism for using a Nazi sympathizer like Musy as a go-between.

Most damaging of all was the fact that some top Nazis were becoming jealous of the Himmler-Musy negotiations. They griped that Himmler was hoarding all the money and favorable publicity instead of sharing it with his cohorts. Eventually, some of them approached Hitler and confronted him with articles about the Himmler-Musy dealings.

As expected, Hitler erupted in one of his monumental furies. "Not a single Jew will leave German soil from now on, as long as I am in charge!" he thundered.

The Musy mission faced collapse. Under this cloud of failure, a third Himmler-Musy meeting produced no results. Mrs. Sternbuch had wanted to accompany Musy and offer her personal intervention, but her husband put his foot down. "If you go along, you might easily be killed, and we can't take that chance. We need you here to help when the war ends–and I need you here always."

She listened and stayed home; and as it turned out, her presence at the meeting would not have made any significant difference. The negotiations came to a halt. The hardliners had carried the day. All promises to release thousands of additional Jews faded into thin air.

ONE LAST CHANCE

It was now clear: As long as Hitler controlled the Nazi war machine, Jews would never be released from the concentration camps. Yet if they could not rescue these Jews for the moment, the Sternbuchs still hoped to save them at the war's end.

This was not as obvious as it seemed. Even as the Allied armies were advancing on Germany during the first months of 1945, the murders of Jews continued in those camps not yet liberated. More ominously, the Nazis began laying down plans to murder every last Jew in their clutches before the Allies could free them. The beasts wanted to remove all possible evidence of their atrocities, and that meant doing away with all potential witnesses, especially camp inmates. Hearing rumors of such plans, the Sternbuchs mobilized their forces to counter them.

Once again they sprang into unabated action. They used the Polish diplomatic pouch to cable reports of last-minute murders of camp inmates to the free world, calling for an international howl of protest. These cables helped lead to the warning delivered by General Eisenhower, the Allied commander in Europe, that heavy punishment would be meted out to any Germans responsible for mistreating those in the camps. Eisenhower's words were printed on millions of leaflets, which were dropped over Germany before the Allied advance into that country. The camp survivors later reported that some Nazi guards treated them a bit less brutally following Eisenhower's message.

The Sternbuchs were also among those who pressed for a policy change from the International Red Cross, which until then had done very little to service Jews held in Nazi captivity. This was especially crucial now, after the Nazis had closed down camps in Eastern Europe to escape the oncoming Russians. The survivors, instead of being freed, were simply dumped into existing camps in the West. As Nazi fortunes declined, there was even less food in the camps to feed twice as many inmates. Starvation was the norm.

At last, shortly before the end of the war, the Red Cross agreed to pass along food packages to these Jews. In some cases, the packages helped inmates hang on until liberation. However, in other camps, the Nazis simply never bothered giving them to the Jews for whom they were intended.

The Sternbuchs' chief initiative at this time was to gain the greatest possible advantage out of their connection with Dr. Musy. Consequently, they urged Musy to continue meeting with Nazi leaders in the hope of securing at least some concessions from them. What frightened the Sternbuchs most were reports that the Nazis stood ready to blow up the concentration camps, with all the inmates still entrapped, as the Allies approached.

"Tell Himmler," the Sternbuchs advised Musy, "that if

the Nazis dare to commit this horrific deed, the world will never, never forgive them. And they had better beware, now that the Allies are only steps away from capturing them."

Musy passed these warnings along, and Himmler got the message. He only asked that, in exchange for his guarantees that the camp inmates would not meet such an end, the Americans agree not to shoot Nazi camp guards on the spot. The Americans eventually consented, and Himmler issued his order: "All Jews in the concentration camp must be handed over peacefully to the Allied armies."

It seemed to secure the inmates' safety. Yet, their welfare was still far from assured, for some camp commanders were unwilling to accept Himmler's decree. They began ordering the starving survivors, not much more than walking skeletons, to leave the camps. They were forced at gunpoint to stagger into the countryside and set out on what became known as "death marches."

As soon as she received word of these latest atrocities, Mrs. Sternbuch rushed to join Musy in Austria, where they met with a Gestapo agent in an effort to halt this breach of Himmler's promise.

Concurrently, Musy's son Benoit set out for a meeting with Nazis in Berlin. He knew that his would be a dangerous mission. Furious battles were raging throughout the devastated city, and communications with the outside world had been virtually cut off. Benoit Musy drove as quickly as he could down the ruined roads, but he wasn't able to avoid Allied gunfire. His car was hit, and the gas tank exploded.

He did not give up. Somehow, he managed to find a mechanic who repaired his car, and he continued on the journey. Eventually he located the Nazi officer he had been seeking, and the officer responded to his arguments by contacting the commanders of the Buchenwald and Bergen-Belsen concentration camps.

"You are to follow Himmler's orders to the letter," he

told them. "The inmates of the camps must be handed over alive."

They were—and so were Jews in two other camps. In all, over one hundred thousand Jewish inmates were transferred alive to the Allied liberators, instead of being shot at the last minute. Among those whose freedom was secured through this agreement was Rabbi Michoel Ber Weissmandl, who had been hiding in a bunker in Slovakia.

The end had finally come for the mad Nazi reign. On April 30, 1945, Hitler committed suicide in his Berlin bunker. One week later, Germany surrendered.

Yet, even with the conclusion of the war, the Sternbuchs' efforts to aid its victims were hardly over.

SERVICING THE SURVIVORS

Those who had survived the indescribable horrors of the camps were alive. But emotionally, physically and spiritually, they very much remained victims. Their frail bodies may have been liberated, but suffering still pervaded their souls. Most were extremely susceptible to disease and depression, and they kept reliving the nightmares of the camp experience. Thus ironically, thousands of inmates who had made it through the war years now fell prey to illness or shock, and died.

Even for those who did not succumb, the war's conclusion brought no panaceas. They had no homes or families to which to return; their parents, wives and children were dead, and their houses had been confiscated by gentiles. For the time being, most of the survivors were sheltered in Displaced Persons Camps, where conditions were generally poor and spirits low. And their spiritual needs were ignored by United Nations workers who were unaware of the role religion played in these Jews' lives.

Once again, the Sternbuchs were in the forefront of

those offering assistance. First, they made good use of their various European contacts to compile lists of survivors and put them in touch with relatives in the free world. Through HIJEFS, they sent packages of sorely needed kosher food, clothing and religious articles. The Jews in Rumania alone received close to fifty thousand dollars in essential aid, a huge sum in those days.

The benefits provided by these packages were often far greater than their immediate value, for they showed the survivors that they had not been forgotten. Their Jewish brothers and sisters in the free world still sought their welfare, reaffirming the links between them. In addition, as one Jewish leader in Poland put it, the parcels of the religious items—the *siddurim, taleisim, tefillin* and candlesticks—reawakened their interest in *Yiddishkeit.* Many of the survivors now began praying in *minyanim* and eating kosher food again, and their faith in Hashem and in humankind was slowly rekindled.

Despite the post-war turmoil, HIJEFS was quickly able to organize relief programs in no fewer than a dozen countries, including Germany, Austria, Italy, Poland, Czechoslovakia, Rumania and Hungary. The small staff of HIJEFS, headed by the very able Mr. Herman Landau and directed by the Sternbuchs, managed to reach out to Jews all over the globe. They were also in constant touch with United Nations personnel who supervised the Displaced Persons Camps, to ensure that the religious needs of the survivors were attended to. Through these contacts, they saw to it that *shuls* and kosher kitchens were eventually established in the camps. For many larger Jewish organizations, HIJEFS became *the* address to contact for information on the survivors during the days of disorder following Germany's surrender.

Mrs. Sternbuch was not content to offer aid from a distance, however. She felt the need to establish a direct, personal connection with the survivors, specifically by visiting them and learning of their needs on a face-to-face basis. A similar trip by Dr. Kuhl and her brother-in-law Eli Sternbuch to Jews in just-liberated camps had garnered valuable lists of survivors and paved the way for her own journeys. However, it was not easy to get around in the hectic months right after the war, since much of Europe had been left in quivering chaos. Finding transportation to make one's way around the shattered countrysides was almost impossible. Nevertheless, given Mrs. Sternbuch's iron will, she usually persevered.

During the end of 1945, and for much of 1946, she was constantly on the move (often joined by her fellow rescue activist Dr. Yaakov Griffel). She kept shuttling from one war-ravaged city to another, bringing precious exit visas to one group of survivors and organizing emergency relief efforts for another. Danger didn't faze her. After scores of Jews were killed in a pogrom in Kielce, Poland, she insisted on visiting the city, despite the obvious threat to her safety.

Her presence in the Displaced Persons Camps brought the survivors not only much-needed goods but, even more importantly, an aura of hope and a sense of comradeship. Those in the drab, gloomy camps greeted her sudden luminous appearance with heartfelt gratitude. She was like a magical benefactress who reminded them that a brighter future lay ahead.

Those at the Zeilsheim camp in Germany were among the many recipients of Mrs. Sternbuch's generosity. She arrived there unheralded one day, lugging suitcases of precious goods. After welcoming her, one of the camp members asked which hotel she would be lodging at during her stay in the area.

"No hotel," Mrs. Sternbuch replied. "I was planning to stay in the camp with you."

"Here? In this place?" The other woman was astounded. "But it's not exactly luxurious here, I'm afraid."

"There are more important things than luxury, my dear. I didn't come to live the life of a queen. I came to be with you."

"Yes, but we aren't able to leave this place. You can; you have a choice."

"Fine. Then I choose to stay with you."

This elegant lady then settled in to live amidst the squalor of the camp and made herself at home among her fellow Jews. She mingled easily with them, listening to their woes, comforting them and promising to seek their early release. Even if she couldn't free them immediately, she told them, she could make their existence easier. She asked people what they needed and compiled lists of their requests. Later, she followed up by sending as many of these goods as she could—even *sheitels* for brides who had asked for them. Some requests were satisfied immediately, for even though she arrived with loaded suitcases, they were always empty when she left. Whatever she had brought along remained behind, to be kept by those she had visited.

"They'll put it to much better use than I would," she said.

HELPING THE LEADERS AND THE YOUNG

Mrs. Sternbuch was especially concerned about the welfare of surviving religious leaders, for they would be charged with rebuilding the religious institutions devastated by war. She sought them out—he *rabbonim*, the teachers, the Bais Yaakov leaders—and offered them aid and support. It was deeply appreciated. One rabbi later commented that Mrs. Sternbuch's encouragement had helped lift his depression and summoned him back to a holier view of life.

Among the many *rabbonim* who benefitted from her financial or diplomatic aid were: the Klausenberger-Sanzer Rav, Rabbi Yekusiel Halberstam; Rabbi Yechiel Weinberg and Rabbi Mordechai Pogramsky, who were offered hospitality and medical care at the Sternbuch home; and the Skulener Rebbe, Rabbi Eliezer Zusia Portugal, whose efforts on behalf

of Jewish orphans in Russia and Rumania received the Sternbuchs' full support.

However, Mrs. Sternbuch's warmest personal attention
was reserved for the youngest and most vulnerable victims of
the war—the children. It was of prime concern to her that
these youngsters, who were often devoid of any memory of
true Jewish life, not be lost to Judaism. They were, after all, the
future, and they constituted the potential proof that the Nazis
had not finally succeeded in cutting the golden cord of Jewish
tradition.

The problems in caring for these children were formidable. Aside from the fact that they had been denied access to
Jewish education during the war, many of the youngsters
were now growing up neglected. They were understandably
distrustful of adults, who had so mistreated them. In addition,
they were maturing in Eastern European countries where the
climate was antithetical to religious growth.

One of Mrs. Sternbuch's first tasks, then, was to try to
spirit the children out of these countries. She could then bring
them to countries like Eretz Yisrael, the United States or
Switzerland, where they could be raised in a free atmosphere
of religious pride.

The governments of Eastern Europe, most of which
were quickly turning Communist, did not take kindly to her
goals. As a result, the Sternbuchs and their associates often
had to resort to daring ruses to obtain the youngsters' release.

One such instance involved a group of Jewish children in
an orphanage in Zakopane, Poland. The orphanage held a
hundred Jewish youngsters under the supervision of Jews
firmly allied to the Communist cause. These diehard leftists
would have nothing to do with any plan to resettle the
orphans in Eretz Yisrael. They threatened to inform the
government if any such attempt was made.

What to do?

As usual, Mrs. Sternbuch brushed aside pessimism and

forged a course of action. She urged young Orthodox activists to visit the orphanage regularly and win the trust of the children and their teachers.

Once that was accomplished, it was time to activate stage two of the plan. The young leaders approached some of the children's teachers and quietly offered them a large sum of money in exchange for their cooperation.

"What would you like us to do?"

"Just tell your supervisors that you want to take the children on a pleasure trip near the border. We'll take over from there."

Permission for the one-day hike was given. The children left the orphanage, and never returned. Instead, they simply kept walking until they reached the border. There, their passage was eased by bribes that made the border guards look the other way. Eventually, the youngsters were brought to an Orthodox children's home in France, where they renewed their acquaintance with their religion.

The scheme was bold and dangerous, but it succeeded. The Communist authorities eventually found out about it, and they reacted furiously. But by then the children were safely beyond their reach. Had they remained under Communist control, they would almost certainly have remained forever bereft of their Jewish identity.

RECLAIMING JEWISH SOULS

In some instances, the children's religious status was challenged on even more direct terms.

During the war, many Jewish orphans had been placed, on a temporary basis, with non-Jewish families. However, after the cessation of hostilities, these non-Jewish foster parents often refused to give up custody of the children. For many youngsters, this meant that they had been baptized and were being brought up as Christians.

To Mrs. Sternbuch and many others, these young help-less Jews being forcibly denied their Jewish heritage was intolerable. She often went from door to door, seeking, pleading and demanding that these Jewish youth be returned to Jewish auspices. It took enormous effort, but with the help of Catholic leaders like Monsignor Bernardini and a sympathetic priest named Pierre Chaillet, she was able to secure an agreement in which HIJEFS assumed custody of many of these children.

However, their return to Jewish circles did not automatically guarantee their return to *Yiddishkeit*. To see that these youngsters received a proper Jewish training, Mrs. Sternbuch and her colleagues helped establish group homes and *yeshivos* for youthful survivors. One such *yeshivah* was set up at Aix-Les-Bains in France under the supervision of Rabbi S. Seil and Rabbi Moshe Lebel, a former student of the Lubliner Rav. Here the youngsters were provided with tailor-made religious instructions that they had earlier been denied.

At first, it was difficult for many of these young survivors, who had experienced so much suffering and cruelty, to respond to their new caretakers' interest. Only gradually did their suspicion melt into trust and their nightmarish memories evolve into dreams of a bright future. Sometimes, though, old recollections of a peaceful pre-war life surfaced. When that occurred, the sight of a glowing *Chanukah menorah* or the sound of a *Shabbos zemirah* could suddenly illuminate lives that had seemed forever darkened. Then the tide would turn, and the slow reapproachment with *Yiddishkeit* would proceed more smoothly. For many, the return became a permanent one. Nothing gave Mrs. Sternbuch and her associates greater satisfaction than watching these young Jews reclaiming their ties to their people.

Once a visitor to one of these children's homes wondered aloud why religion played such a prominent role in the home's activities. The educational director Mrs. Shifra Yudasin replied, "Well, don't forget that the children here are orphans. They have been deprived of their fathers by the Nazis. So we must see to it that they indeed gain a father–their Heavenly Father."

By the time the last Displaced Persons Camps were dismantled in the early 1950s, most of these orphans had begun building new lives in Eretz Yisrael, the United States or Western Europe. Today, many of them are among the most dedicated and productive members of world Jewry. Their contributions to Judaism stand as a tribute to the valiant workers who struggled so hard to win their release from isolation and ignorance.

FINAL SATISFACTIONS

Mrs. Sternbuch also rejoiced in watching her own children grow up committed to the ideals and practices of authentic Judaism. Her son Rabbi Avraham Sternbuch became the head of the Bobover Yeshivah in London, her older daughter Netty married Rabbi Chaim Segal, principal of Mesivta Rabbi Chaim Berlin in Brooklyn, and her younger daughter Esther became the wife of Rabbi Yehudah Gutterman, dean of the junior Yeshivas Ponevezh in Bnei Brak. In addition, all her grandchildren lengthened the chain of tradition by devoting themselves to Torah study at *yeshivos* and *kollelim* throughout the world.

Recha Sternbuch passed away in 1971, shortly after the death of her beloved husband, who had always lovingly supported and aided her projects. Because she always insisted on avoiding honors, her name did not become familiar to the general Jewish public during her lifetime.

Yet, her incredible acts of courage continue to reverberate throughout Jewish history, as indications of what one dedicated woman can do for the sake of her fellow Jews. She was truly a heroine for all time and an *eishes chayil*, a woman of valor, in every sense of the word.

THE TANGIERS CONNECTION

MRS RENEE REICHMANN

Renee Reichmann, a refugee mother of six from Vienna, working from her new home in Tangiers with the help of her daughter Eva, sent many thousands of food packages to Jews in the camps, including Auschwitz. She also provided protective papers for over twelve hundred Jews in Budapest.

6   THE TANGIERS CONNECTION

MRS. RENEE REICHMANN

"ATTENTION! UP IMMEDIATELY, YOU LAZY GARBAGE!"

The atmosphere in the camp barracks, already unbearable, was instantly seared with tension. The haunted eyes of the women inmates turned towards the insufferable face of the *kapo*. She was brandishing her usual superior sneer. Would she dare be so boldly insolent without the SS guard behind her? they wondered.

They struggled to their blistered feet and waited for the newest dreaded announcement. What atrocity had they committed now? Had someone dared steal a crumb of bread? Tried to rest between assignments? Had the awful audacity to act human? And which of them would be tortured for that?

The *kapo* blared out her words. "Number 173049! Come forward!"

There was a stir, but no one spoke up. No one even looked around. They would not betray their fellow inmate with an identifying glance.

"I'll say it one more time," the *kapo* screamed. "Number

173049! This is your last chance. Next time, I will have the number retired. Permanently."

From the group, an emaciated figure stumbled forward. The gauntness of her face was accentuated by her shorn head. What had once been sparkling eyes were now hollow. What had once been a vibrant young Jewish woman was now a resigned zombie. The weeks in the camp had aged her by decades.

"You are Number 173049, named Meiselman?"

"Yes," she whispered.

"Next time, answer immediately when called. Or else."

Next time? Chaya Meiselman laughed inwardly. She knew there would never be a next time.

"Come with me," the *kapo* declared.

Instinctively, Chaya drew back. "But I haven't done anything. Why do I have to go?"

"I am not interested in your life story. I have orders to take you to the Commandant's office. Walk!"

Chaya knew it was no use arguing. There was never any logic in a Nazi's sense of "logic." As had happened to so many others, her life would be taken for no reason at all.

For a brief instant, she scanned the faces of the other Jewish women in the barracks. Silently, through the pain etched on their faces, they conveyed their comradeship and their sympathy at her plight. Another one was being taken away. So many were gone already, but each loss was a tragedy all its own. Their fear kept them silent, but their eyes expressed their feelings. She, in turn, nodded slightly in acknowledgment. They had, after all, been her surrogate family during these nightmarish days. She would miss them.

She followed the *kapo* silently, struggling to keep up with the other's sharp march. She was led to the Commandant's office and ordered inside. To what would she be forced to confess, she wondered. When would the torture begin? She closed her eyes and began murmuring the *Shema*.

Suddenly, a burly man in full military uniform stomped into the room. He circled the solitary Jewish woman and then, smiling fiendishly, plopped himself down behind his desk.

"So you are Chaya Meiselman, right?"

"Yes, sir." Her eyes remained downcast.

"How long have you been at the camp here?"

She paused to consider. "I . . . I'm afraid I've lost track of time."

"Do you still remember your old life outside the camp?"

"Yes, a bit." More than a bit, of course. She dreamed about it all the time, as long as her senses could bear it.

"Too bad. I thought we'd made you forget about all that by now."

The Nazi chuckled. Chaya was still bewildered. What was this all about? Why didn't he stop teasing her and get to the point?

Then the Nazi composed himself and went on. "Well, it seems the outside world hasn't forgotten you. You apparently still have friends out there, though I'd hoped we'd done away with them. But someone decided to send you this."

The Nazi reached behind him and produced a bulky package. Chaya glanced at the address label, and indeed, it bore her name. Still, she hesitated to take it. She'd been well-trained by now not to take things at face value.

The Nazi noticed her reluctance. "What's the matter? Do you think there's a bomb inside?" His fat sides heaved with laughter. "We don't need bombs. We have other ways of dealing with you Jews."

Then, like a mild day turned stormy, he suddenly grew threatening. "I've wasted enough time with you. Hurry up! If the Red Cross didn't make us deliver these, I'd keep them myself and use them for my dogs."

He made Chaya sign an acknowledgment of receipt and then ordered her back to her barracks.

She clutched the package tightly as she reentered the

overcramped quarters. The others regarded her with awe, as if she were a ghost tantalizing their sense of reality. How was it that she was still alive and unharmed? Then they saw the package. Whispers accumulated throughout the room.

"What?"

"Why?"

"How?"

Chaya had nothing to tell them.

Slowly, she removed the packaging, as the others crowded around. It wasn't a bomb but a bombshell. Inside were morsels of food that seemed like a mirage, sardines, almonds, raisins and pieces of choice chocolate, ten pounds' worth in all. Items that had once been taken for granted and that now glittered like gold. And they would truly be worth a fortune when traded to the *kapos* for lifesaving favors.

Thanking Hashem, Chaya offered to share her treasure with the others. She could afford to be generous, now that someone had been so generous to her. Her doubts could now be laid to rest. Someone in the outside world still cared about what happened to her, still wanted her to live. It gave her the will to do so.

But who was this unknown patron? Who had taken such time, effort and expense to make such a benevolent gesture?

The neatly printed return address on the package indicated that it had been sent from Tangiers, Spanish Morocco, in northern Africa. And the name read, in block letters, "Mrs. Renee Reichmann."

Like many of those to whom Mrs. Reichmann was a benefactress, Chaya Meiselman had never heard of her. Yet Chaya, along with thousands of others, had abundant reason to be eternally grateful for this unique woman's courageous generosity. Along with her ever-helpful daughter Eva, Renee Reichmann managed to sustain many a concentration camp inmate just when their morale was at its lowest ebb. They provided incontestable proof that the concentration camp inmates had by no means been forgotten by their fellow Jews around the world.

ON THE RUN

Renee Reichmann's life bore many similarities to that of her colleague in rescue work Recha Sternbuch. She, too, was the daughter of a *talmid chacham*, Rabbi Avraham Gestetner, who hailed from Hungary. And as the eldest of twelve children, she learned early on the responsibility of caring for others.

Like Mrs. Sternbuch, Renee Reichmann enjoyed a prosperous pre-war life as the wife of a successful businessman. Her husband Shmaya (Samuel) built up a wholesale egg distribution enterprise in Beled, Hungary, and together they raised a sizable family of one daughter and five sons. The eldest of the children, a daughter named Eva, would eventually become her mother's indispensable assistant in *hatzalah* activities.

The Reichmanns left Hungary after an attempted Communist coup in 1918 and moved to Vienna, where Mrs. Reichmann's *chessed* activities were legion. She was especially noted for assisting patients who came to the Austrian capital for medical treatment.

After ten years there, the Reichmanns' placid existence was shattered by the Anschluss, which forced a union between Germany and Austria. As the conquering Nazi soldiers goosestepped down Vienna's broad boulevards, the Reichmanns, along with Austria's other Jews, realized that their human rights could no longer be taken for granted. The convulsions of Kristallnacht in November, 1938, only confirmed their worst fears. It was time to leave Vienna, and the Reichmanns saw only one natural destination–Eretz Yisrael, the Jews' ancient homeland.

Mr. Reichmann frantically tried to gain certificates of entry to the Holy Land. Yet, despite his varied connections, all his efforts were futile. The British, the official nemesis of the Nazis, controlled entry to Palestine, and they vigilantly guarded its portals, especially against Jews trying to enter. Every request for certificates was turned down. The Reichmanns would have to look for refuge elsewhere.

The war was already in progress, prompting a desperate gamble. Leaving behind almost everything they owned, they escaped to Paris in mid-1940. But this hardly guaranteed safety, for the Nazis were right behind them. When France fell to the Germans in June, 1940, the Reichmanns joined other refugees in fleeing to the French-Spanish border.

A French policeman sympathetic to their situation gave them some advice. "You'd better leave French soil immediately. You know what the Nazis will do when they find you, and don't count on the French to protect you, either."

The suggestion was sound, but it, too, posed problems. The only direction left open to them was across the border into Spain. But as they were well aware, Spain, though officially neutral in the war, was a virtual ally of Hitler. Germany had supported Spain's leader General Francisco Franco in his victorious civil war against the Russian-backed Loyalist forces in 1936. Spain, therefore, did not promise to be hospitable for Jews. If neutral Switzerland, having no alliance with Hitler, was actively keeping Jews from entering, Spain would undoubtedly turn them away, too.

Having no choice, though, the Reichmanns made the move. They obtained a ten-day transit visa and prepared to cross into Spain. Mr. Reichmann decided to precede the others, reasoning that it would be easier for a single individual to obtain entry than for an entire family. Once inside the country, he could assist the others.

Coming to the border guards, he produced the visa and requested permission to enter the country. They gave their quick and unconditional approval.

Emboldened, he went further. "As you can see from my papers, I have a family. Can they cross the border too?" He held his breath.

"You want to go get your family and bring them here, too?" The officials pondered for a moment. "Well, there might be a problem with that."

"Yes? What?"

"They have to be here by six o'clock tonight."

"And if they're not?"

"Then . . ."

"Yes?"

"Then they'll have to come back tomorrow morning, because six o'clock is when we close."

Shmaya Reichmann didn't risk the delay. He called his family immediately, and they joined him before the day was up.

However, as their papers were being examined, a true problem cropped up. It was one they'd expected but had hoped to avoid. While in France, they'd come across Talia, a Hungarian girl who had left her homeland in flight from the Nazis. With the Nazis moving in on Paris, and without anyone to turn to for protection, she had been on the verge of hysteria.

The Reichmanns felt a surge of sympathy for this fellow Jewish refugee.

"Would you like to travel with us?" they offered. "We're setting out for Spain. Please come along."

"But I don't have any passport or visas," she said.

"From now on, you'll be part of our family. Eva always wanted a sister."

It was a noble sentiment, but it was about to meet its ultimate test.

The border officials perused their documents again and again and then stared up at them. The Reichmanns could presume what was passing through their minds. Their passport listed six children, and he had obviously counted seven.

They had to make a firm decision, and they did without debate. If the official challenged Talia's entry, they would fight it. And if she were denied permission to move on, they would stay with her.

Finally, the senior official cleared his throat and approached Mr. Reichmann. "There seems to be some mistake here."

"I know, but . . ."

"The passport lists only six children."

"Yes. However . . ."

"Clumsy passport people. If someone has seven children, then they should say so. I'll make sure everything is cleared up. You can move on."

Mr. Reichmann wasn't sure he'd heard right. "Everything is all right?"

"What could be wrong?" said the official. "We're here to be helpful, aren't we?" He gave Mr. Reichmann a warm smile and a wink, and placed the papers back into his hands.

THE TANGIERS PROJECT

The Reichmanns, together with Talia, were now safely within Spain's borders. Their puzzlement persisted, though. Why was a country so clearly aligned with Hitler being so accommodating to Hitler's sworn enemies? The question became a prime topic of hushed conversation among the Jews in Spain.

Some suggested that Spain was just reciprocating for France's having taken in refugees during the Spanish Civil War. Others whispered that Spain's fascist dictator Francisco Franco was favorably disposed towards Jews due to personal considerations. He was really a descendant of Marranos, those

Spanish Jews who had outwardly converted to Christianity in the Middle Ages but who had maintained fealty to Jewish traditions in secret. Whatever the case, the Reichmanns were grateful Hashem had pointed them towards a haven.

Still, Spain was located in the sphere of war activity and might not provide long-standing safety. The Reichmanns decided to move on to Tangier, a city in Spanish Morocco, located in North Africa. Because Spanish Morocco is located directly south of Spain, beyond the Rock of Gibralter, passage there proved relatively easy. Furthermore, Tangier played host to a community of several thousand Sephardic Jews, and *kashrus* and *minyanim* were readily available there.

Soon after arriving there, Mrs. Reichmann received a letter from an old Viennese acquaintance. The woman, now living in the United States, was a member of the Klein family, members of which eventually founded the Bartons Candy firm.

The letter came straight to the point: "My in-laws are still trapped in Poland, suffering severe privations. With the war on, it's almost impossible to send them help from America. Could you manage to ship food packages to them from Tangier? Enclosed is their address. Please do anything you can."

Mrs. Reichmann responded immediately. She assembled a neatly-arrayed package of delicacies and shipped it out to the designated address. She was glad to assist in this essential *mitzvah*, especially since it had been so simple to perform.

Some time later, the postman called. He was returning the by-now dented package. When Mrs. Reichmann asked him what had happened, he simply pointed to the notification scrawled on the front: "Cannot be delivered. Addressee deported to Auschwitz."

PACKAGES OF CARE

The chilling bluntness of this development stunned her at first. Even a righteous person dedicated to helping others might have succumbed now to second thoughts: "Well, I tried, but what can I do?"

Renee Reichmann saw it differently. True, she had been too late to send the parcel to the Jews' home. But who said she couldn't forward it to them at the concentration camp itself?

And if she could get one package through to the deprived Jews, then why not two? Why not a hundred? Why not, indeed?

Yet, how could she reach out to these masses if she didn't know who they were? The Nazis would never allow items to be delivered to Jewish masses in general. But if she could find out the names of specific Jews sent to the concentration camps, then perhaps . . .

For help, she turned to her brother Hesky Gestetner, a Jewish communal leader in Bratislava, Slovakia. He responded by sending her the names and destinations of eighteen hundred Jews who had been sent to Nazi labor camps. Most of these were young women from Slovakia who were among the first Jews deported to Auschwitz-Birkenau.

She began writing to these inmates and getting responses. But it now became clear that the parcel-shipping process could no longer be a one-woman project. Sending packages to nearly two thousand individuals required both additional funds and dedicated assistants. Renee Reichmann set out to acquire both.

She began by visiting homes and businesses, and establishing contacts. Mrs. Reichmann was armed with the knowledge that many Moroccan Jews had established flourishing businesses and were in a sound position to help.

"Life might be good for you here," her pitch went. "But think of those defenseless Jews wasting away in those horrible

Nazi labor camps. A food package might keep them alive for a day, or a week, or a month. Long enough to survive the winter and beyond."

"Sounds like a good cause," was a typical response. "I'll think about it for a while."

"A while can be an eternity if you're in a labor camp," she would counter. "Do you really think these people can wait?"

"Maybe not. But how do you know these Jews will get the packages anyway? Who says the Nazis won't confiscate them?"

"We know that most of them are getting through," Mrs. Reichmann replied. "That's because we're getting postcards from the Jews saying they've received them. The relatives we've shown these cards to have confirmed the signatures. So we're hopeful."

The businessmen were intrigued. "Do you mean these prisoners are writing back to their relatives in Europe?"

"No. That would be too risky. They're afraid the Nazis would find out where their relatives are and arrest them. Instead, they're sending the cards here to Tangier, where the Nazis can't reach. And according to the cards, the packages are extremely helpful to them. They can trade the things we send them for some extra food or a little lighter assignment from the guards."

"I'm surprised the Nazis are letting them write cards at all."

"Don't you see?" Mrs. Reichmann drove home the point. "It's part of the Nazi propaganda effort. They want to make the rest of the world believe Jews in the camps are being treated well. But if you read between the lines, you can tell that the Jews are being terrorized beyond belief. That's why we have to step up our campaign for them even more. And we'd better do it now, while the Spanish government is letting us send out the goods. They might say they hate the Jews, but they sometimes act like our best friends."

The businessmen were convinced. They joined the campaign and directed their friends to do likewise. With the assistance of the Tangier Jewish community, the package project grew significantly.

However, it was not only the wealthy who helped out. Mrs. Reichmann also secured the active assistance of youngsters in the neighborhood, including her own children.

Her teenage sons spent their after-school hours packing the assorted foods, usually compact, healthful items such as nuts, raisins and sardines, and loading them onto trucks that would bring them to the railroads for delivery.

Sixteen-year-old Eva Reichmann was an equal partner with her mother in all these activities, a young devoted person whose knowledge of Spanish was especially useful in dealing with government officials.

Soon, the project had received international recognition. As was the case throughout the war, other Orthodox rescue organizations, rather than considering Mrs. Reichmann a rival, pledged their full support for her efforts and ensured it a major niche in the Orthodox *hatzalah* network. The Vaad Hatzalah made Mrs. Reichmann its Tangier representative and supplied her with thousands of dollars. Through Recha Sternbuch in Switzerland, the Vaad also sent her priceless lists containing names of Jews who would benefit from her packages. Yet, the Vaad was not the only source of information or aid. Mrs. Reichmann gratefully accepted the assistance of any individual and always agreed to send a package to any needy Jew, regardless of his or her background.

By 1943, some four thousand packages were being shipped out every other week to Jews living under the Nazis' heel.

RIGHTEOUS GENTILES

The efforts of just the Jews working with Mrs. Reichmann would not have been enough to ensure success, though. The packages had to pass through foreign countries on their way to their destinations. Had the authorities in these lands refused to allow passage, the entire project would have been doomed.

Here, too, Heaven smiled upon the venture. Mrs. Reichmann and Eva went to Spanish officials, hoping to win their consent for the shipping plans.

"Your excellencies, this might seem presumptuous, but we need your permission to ship food parcels from here to Jews in German-occupied lands. We're not sending out arms or ammunition, only simple packages of food stuffs. We brought one here for you to examine."

One of the officials took up her suggestion. After going through the goods, he nodded. "I must say one thing. I am not a big admirer of Jews, but I will grant you this. You Jews clearly help each other out. I am sure we can convince our German friends that allowing these packages into Poland shouldn't be a problem."

Mrs. Reichmann was gratified. "We deeply appreciate your humanitarian help. If only there were more like you."

"But there are. Have you met the head of the Spanish Red Cross? There's a true humanitarian. I will put you in touch with him."

El Conde de la Granja was the grandiose name of this noted diplomat. The Reichmanns approached him somewhat timidly, but to their surprise he proved to be very much down to earth in his concern for the camp inmates.

"As a matter of fact, we recognize the Jews in the concentration camps as prisoners of war," he told them. "As such, they deserve to be treated properly."

In this, he and his associates compared most favorably to

the heads of the International Red Cross. This supposedly unbiased, humanitarian-minded group did not recognize Jews in the camps as prisoners of war until 1944, and even then only because of the pressure emanating from George Mantello's press campaign. De la Granja was much more sympathetic.

"By all means, send the packages in our name if that will help," he informed the Reichmanns.

They were more than happy to do so. By working under the auspices of the Spanish Red Cross, they were able to send the packages without paying prohibitive postage fees, since the Spanish government absorbed the expenses. This saved them a significant amount of money, enabling them to ship out many additional parcels. The Spanish Red Cross helped in other ways as well. When Mrs. Reichmann's sons arrived at the Red Cross offices with some fifeen hundred packages to be shipped out, the official in charge didn't burden them with bureaucratic red tape.

"Here, use this official stamp instead of writing the organization's name on each one," he said. "That should speed things up. And make sure you mark Prisoner of War on every package. That will help guarantee that they'll reach their destination. Tell me, how many packages do you have in all?"

"About fifteen hundred. We can give you the exact count as soon as possible."

"Don't bother. We'll take your word for it. Better get started. You have a lot of work to do. Good luck!"

The Reichmanns also managed at times to send parcels under the auspices of the International Red Cross. However, since the I.R.C. did not direct packages to specific Jews, only to concentration camp Jews in general, it was difficult to gain acknowledgment of the parcels' receipt. To make matters worse, the I.R.C. sometimes refused to pass along the goods, because "the chocolate inside isn't up to the high Swiss standards." As if the starving camp inmates would be so choosy in their tastes.

BEYOND JUST FOOD

The scope of the Reichmanns' activities continued to expand, bolstered by the steady flow of aid from Vaad Hatzalah, relayed through Recha Sternbuch. Eventually, the Joint Distribution Committee added its vast resources to the campaign, through its Tangier representative Isaac Lorado. Mr. Lorado helped secure the assistance of a fellow Sephardic merchant in Tangier named Aaron Cohn, who provided the Reichmanns with a spacious warehouse for storing the goods to be sent. By 1944, with thousands of parcels being prepared every week, the Reichmanns were able to vary their contents. They now contained not only everyday nutritional needs, but also clothing and, for *Pesach* of 1944, *matzos*. Thus, some fortunate Jews were able to hold an abbreviated but profoundly moving *seder* inside Birkenau itself in 1944.

At this very juncture, the Jews of Hungary became direct targets of the fading Nazis' fury. The killing machine was revved up to full throttle, as the butchers sought to annihilate as many of this last large Jewish community as possible before the war ended. Deportations and gassings were stepped up in a race to finish off these Jews before the coming liberation.

Mrs. Reichmann heard reports of these atrocities in a growing state of revulsion. At the same time, she learned of the usefulness of the Latin American papers held by numerous Jews in Nazi-occupied lands. Those who possessed these documents, like the Salvadoran papers given out by George Mantello, were usually protected from Nazi atrocities.

Could additional documents be distributed? And could additional Jews be saved through them? Mrs. Reichmann was determined to make the attempt.

She wrote to Mrs. Sternbuch in Switzerland, as well as to Chaim Roth in Hungary. The message was terse but urgent. "I need names of Jews in danger, Jewish children targeted for the camps. If I can get them entry permits to Tangier through my connections, they might be rescued."

The names of some five hundred Hungarian children and seventy adults who would accompany them arrived within days.

Next, she met with J. Rives Childes, the *charge d'affaires* of the American Legation of Tangier.

"Senor Childs, I thank you for your time. I am here not on behalf of myself, but on behalf of five hundred desperate Jewish children. They are being rounded up daily, and soon, if no one helps them, they will be shipped to death camps to become only memories of great promise. But if they can be given some official documents, some entry permits to Tangier, the Nazis might think twice about deporting them. Can anything be done?"

Mr. Childs, a refined individual and a naturally benevolent man, had an immediate reply. "I've had some fruitful dealings with General Luis Orgaz, the Spanish High Commissioner for Tangier. He has quite a bit of influence in matters of immigration. I have a feeling he would be able to help."

"Can you possibly see him on our behalf?"

"Absolutely."

General Orgaz approved the visas without any prodding. The Reichmanns then rushed to furnish the children with them, with beneficial results. Those youngsters holding the visas were spirited to safe houses in Budapest, living under the protection of the Spanish Red Cross. There they remained unharmed until the war's end, spared the fate of so many of their peers.

That, however, was not all. In the interim, Mrs. Reichmann had received the names of seven hundred additional children. Perhaps they, too, could be saved. But would Mr.

Childs and General Orgaz be willing to put themselves out for her again?

Mrs. Reichmann didn't fret over possible rejection. She set off with one of her sons to once again seek the officials' aid. Her daughter Eva was apprehensive.

"If we ask for too much, they might turn us down and we'll be left with nothing. Maybe we should ask for just a hundred visas this time."

Mrs. Reichmann was aghast. "Don't ever think small!" she exhorted her daughter. "Once we're there, we'll ask for the full seven hundred visas. That way, they might feel inclined to give us half–still a lot more than a hundred. We can't be timid with these children's lives."

Mrs. Reichmann's suggestion was adopted. The request for seven hundred visas was made.

Soon the response arrived: "All seven hundred visas are yours." Once again, the Spanish government had come through.

Like the earlier group, the recipients of these papers were also granted protection. They, too, survived the war.

In actuality, those who escaped death by means of the exit visas may have numbered as many as three thousand. The Spanish Ambassador to Hungary left instructions that any other Jews who wished to receive visas be granted them, and many Jews availed themselves of this offer. Other Jews, noting the effectiveness of these papers, forged their own copies. The Spanish also provided protected houses in Budapest, like those set up by Raoul Wallenberg of Sweden, where Hungarian Jews could stay without being accosted.

MATRIARCH SUPREME

Even after the Nazis' defeat, the Reichmanns' devotion to Jewish war victims persisted. With confusion and starvation plaguing Europe, their assistance was as providential as ever, and perhaps more so. Due to bureaucratic restrictions imposed by the victorious Allies, private organizations found it almost impossible to go to Europe to help the survivors.

The Reichmanns' food package campaign, though, was an exception, since it was based in Tangier, outside Europe. Their operation had been humming along so efficiently that the Allies allowed it to continue. Even the potent Joint Distribution Committee relied on them to reach the remnants of European Jewry. When France was liberated from Nazi control in 1944, JDC representatives asked the Reichmanns to send parcels to French Jews on their behalf. They knew the Reichmanns could process and send them more effectively than anyone else. The packages kept coming until a semblance of order was reestablished in Europe and other Jewish organizations were allowed to set up their own relief systems over a year later.

The Reichmann family eventually moved from Tangier to Canada in the late 1950s, establishing a tile import company there. Its success led them to pursue ventures in the real estate and construction fields. Soon the Reichmann sons had become the heads of the firm, which prospered phenomenally.

They used their money wisely to aid their fellow humans. At the same time, the Reichmann sons remain devoted to their religion and its precepts. Secular newspapers like the *Wall Street Journal* marvel in print about these Orthodox Jews who run a vast business empire but still take time out to recite *tefillos*. The Reichmann sons have become world renowned for both the vastness of their philanthropy and their low-key approach to charity-giving. Without major fanfare, they support many Torah institutions throughout the world, helping to secure the revival of the traditional Judaism that Hitler had worked so hard to destroy.

Eva passed away in 1986, and her beloved mother four years later, in February, 1990, at the age of 91. She had lived a long and fulfilling life and had been blessed with the opportunity to see her offspring thrive by continuing her magnanimous work. Their success was not surprising, for they had a magnificent role model to inspire their devotion to helping others.

CONCLUSION

"*BE'MAKOM SHE'AIN ISH, HISHTADEL LIHIYOS ISH,*" SAID THE
sage Rabban Gamliel. "Where no other leader is present, do
your best to assume the role." (*Avos* 2:5) Where no one else
acts to meet a crisis, one must assume the responsibility
oneself.

The men and women profiled in this book did just that.
They cast aside their everyday professions and identities and
took on tasks normally left to international movers and shak-
ers. For the duration of the war, and even beyond, they filled
the vacuum left by the uncaring, the timid and the inflexible;
they threw themselves into rescue work with full body and
soul in order to fulfill the Torah's dictum of the rescue of
endagered Jews as the highest priority. And where earlier
they might have lived quietly within the confines of their
small communities, they suddenly emerged as whirlwinds of
activity, communicating with diplomats and world leaders,
and touching–and rescuing–the lives of fellow Jews thousands of miles away. Their bond with the community of world

Jewry proved to be stronger than all the forces their opponents hurled against them.

We pray that Hashem will grant us only peace and prosperity in the future. Yet, if crises occur, may He also grant us the strength to avoid the errors of the past and to learn from the examples of those who aided their endangered brothers and sisters regardless of any obstacles—and we pray that we be imbued with the Torah perspective of concern for each and every Jew.

They rose above petty rivalries and self-interest to focus on the ultimate priority—saving lives. In the process, they achieved a world of good, and their actions made a world of difference.

ABOUT THE AUTHORS

Dr. David Kranzler, historian and full professor (ret.) at CUNY, is the author of five books on the Holocaust, including: *Japanese, Nazis and Jews: The Jewish Refugee Community of Shanghai 1938-1945, Heroine of Rescue* (with Joseph Friedensohn) and *Thy Brother's Blood: The Orthodox Jewish Response during the Holocaust.* Dr. Kranzler is presently completing two works: *The Greatest Hero of the Holocaust: the Man Who Stopped Deportations from Budapest to Auschwitz* and a biography of Reb Elimelech Tress.

Rabbi Eliezer Gevirtz, an editor of the *Darkeinu* and *Zeirei Forum* magazines and frequent contributor to *Olomeinu Magazine*, is the author of *The Story of the Chafetz Chaim* (co-authored with Rabbi Nosson Scherman) and *Lehovin Ulehaskil.* Rabbi Gevirtz resides in the Washington Heights section of New York City and teaches at both Yeshiva Rabbi Samson Raphael Hirsch in Manhattan and the S\A\R Academy in Riverdale.

ACKNOWLEDGMENTS

RABBI DAVID KRANZLER

MY SINCEREST APPRECIATION TO THREE TRULY GOOD FRIENDS: Ernest Seewald, Al Lipson and Rebbitzin Judith Grunfeld, who were so very helpful in so many different ways.

My personal debt to all the heroes and heroines of rescue for serving as inspiration of *mesiras nefes* on behalf of *Klal Yisrael* for me and my family.

I would like to express my deepest gratitude to *Hakadosh Baruch Hu*, Who has enabled me to concentrate on my life-long ambition to research and relate the history of the great Torah-imbued rescue heroes of yesteryear. Their great exploits have been neglected or distorted, wittingly and unwittingly, by secularist historians, who cannot tolerate any disturbance of their preconceived and distorted stereotype of the real Torah Jew.

Dr. David Kranzler
Brooklyn, New York
Shvat 5751 (1991)

ACKNOWLEDGMENTS

RABBI ELIEZER GEVIRTZ

THE OVERRIDING INSPIRATION FOR THIS VOLUME CAME FROM the subjects themselves, the remarkable activists whose self-less efforts during the Holocaust proved just how effective individual rescue initiatives could be. Their allegiance to the Torah precepts of *hatzalah* (rescue) and *areivus* (responsibility) was manifested on a superhuman scale, with results that benefitted many thousands of their fellow Jews. May their holy examples continue to spur us on to achieve the seemingly impossible, both during times of crisis and in our daily search for spiritual improvement.

We are humbly grateful to *Hakadosh Baruch Hu*, Who in His supreme kindness and generosity has enabled us to honor those who so richly deserve the recognition of their fellow Jews.

Rabbi Eliezer Gevirtz
New York City
Shvat 5751 (1991)